ADOPTED BY THE STREETS

TYVON PRICE

PAGE PUBLISHING, INC.
New York, NY

First originally published by Page Publishing, Inc. 2019

ISBN 978-1-64544-262-2 (Paperback)
ISBN 978-1-64544-263-9 (Digital)

Printed in the United States of America

INTRODUCTION

Turning twenty-five in a man's life is special, makes us feel like we've become a *real* man. But turning twenty-five in Richmond, California, is a blessing. See, Richmond is a place where kings and queens are made, and at the same time it's also a place that is cursed. Growing up in Richmond, you are taught the rules of surviving the streets at young age. All depending on who your parents are, you will be set up to fail or set up to succeed. Some parents pass down generational blessings to their kids, and most pass down the generational curses. This story I tell you is not to show you how bad Richmond is; it's to show you how being raised in the hood can help you become successful, or it can cause you to become a statistic in the environment you were raised in. It's pretty much on you and the choices you decide to make. If you from the hood, you often feel like you ain't choose this life, this life chose you.

Chapter 1

Wake Up!

Boom! Boom! Boom!

"Aye! Wake up, nigga, some suckas just slid through and hit that nigga Twan outside!" Lil Donny yells.

Lil Donny is my little brother, six years younger than me.

"I told you they was gone catch that nigga slippin' for snitchin' on Uncle Stino. Where my five?"

Lil Donny rolls his eyes while pulling out the five he owe me.

"Now close my door and wake me up when the ambulance come, so I can find out how many times them niggas hit him."

"Bra, Mommy says do y'all want to eat this morning?" my twin brother Bobby say to us, peeking through the door I just asked Donny to close. Bobby is my twin.

"What she cook?" I ask, still lying in the bed.

"Nigga, do you want some or not?"

"Yeah, I do. Now close my door when y'all leave."

Both of them walk off without closing the door. Having brothers can sometimes be a pain in the ass, I thought as I got up to close it. I look out the window to see Twan, a twenty-four-year-old boy who just had a brand-new born baby boy. He was dead. Laid out there on the ground, gone.

I decided to get dressed and go eat so I can finally be headed to school.

"Look, boys, y'all be careful out there today when y'all get out of school. Y'all know niggas gone be trippin' over Twan getting knocked down."

My mama stands in the middle of the kitchen saying this as she stares at a us with a concerned look.

"Well, he shouldn't have never snitched on Unc, that's what that nigga get," Bobby says.

"Boy, Shut up. Twan knew y'all wen y'all was babies, y'all all played together," Mama says, a bit irritated at the fact her son would even say something that rude.

We all turn our heads because the front door opens.

"Man, fuck that nigga. He can snitch on dirt now," Bobby says.

"Lil nigga, you betta watch how you talk to yo moms before I bust you in yo mouth," Uncle Stino says.

Uncle Stino was my dad's best friend. He and my dad ran the streets of Richmond till one day some hating-ass nigga set my dad up for a hit, dropped fifty bands on his head. They say it was the south side who set it up. My pops was from north. Back then it was a peaceful place of getting money. The focus was on the bag, but when my dad died, it turned into a war zone over streets. Friends turn against friends, even family snaked one another. In Richmond, it was kill or be killed.

Ever since my dad died when I was ten, my Uncle Stino was the one who helped Moms raise us. He taught us the street life even though Moms did not like it. He said he was preparing us for the game that they was raised in.

I wasn't really ready to sell dope at twelve. Shit, I barely even knew how to multiply at that age. But let me tell you, the first drop I did and the amount I made out off of it changed my whole frame of mind. I was like, fuck school, sign me up to be a gangsta. It was all about the hustle, and because of who my uncle and my pops was, it wasn't on me, it was in me.

My brother Bobby was with it as soon as my uncle Stino introduced it to him. See, Bobby is the opposite of me he is very hot-headed and says whatever is on his mind. It doesn't matter if you like it or not. He is a troublemaker, and he's always getting me involved in something whether it's helping him in a fight or lying for him to get him out of trouble. That's my brother though, and I am my brother's keeper.

My youngest brother Donny, everybody calls him Lil D. You can blame Bobby for that nickname because one hot summer day at the community pool Bobby decides to pull his pants down right on the diving board in front of tons of people, which created the name Lil D.

Donny is a smart little guy. I'll say even smarter then Bobby. Bobby tends to pick on Donny a lot as a big brother should, but it's funny how Donny outsmarts Bobby and gets him in trouble with Mom. For example, it was one time when Lil D was watching TV, and Bobby came home with some friends, and they started picking on Lil D. He ran to the corner and balled up, acting as if he were crying, so that made Bobby and his friends want to talk about him. More like calling him all types of names like "Cry Baby," "Lil dick," "Inky Binky." That's when Donny came out, his ball with his phone in his hand and Mama on speakerphone. I can tell you Bobby and his friends didn't sit on their ass right the whole week.

Back at breakfast. "I told that boy to watch his mouth. It's gone get him in trouble one of these days," Mama says.

"Too late for that," Lil D says sarcastically.

Bobby slaps Lil D in the back of the head and chuckles. Unc Stino slaps Bobby in the back of the head, and everybody chuckles.

"Leave yo lil brother alone," Unc Stino says.

"So, Unc Stino, did you really have that nigga Twan hit?" Bobby says while scratching his head.

"Boy, hush and mind your own business, kid. Stay out of grown folks' business," Mama says.

"I am grown," Bobby says.

Everybody laughs once again.

"I don't know what y'all laughing at. I got all the new J's and all the new gear, all the girls bc on me at school."

"Boy, that don't make you grown, it just makes you look like a clown wearing all that stuff and don't even know how to read properly," Mama says.

Bobby pulls out a stack of money and says, "I know how to count, that's good enough for me."

Mama rolls her eyes. Unc Stino chuckles and says, "Boy, you remind me so much of your father, it's a damn shame."

"Y'all gone and get ready for school before y'all be late," Mama says.

Before getting up from the table, Bobby asks Uncle Stino, "So what's up, you laid that nigga down or what?"

Uncle Stino doesn't say anything, he just winks at him with a sly grin.

Bobby runs down the hall saying, "I told y'all niggas Unc did that shit like a G."

"Why you telling that boy all that nonsense? You know he got a big mouth?" Mama asks Stino.

"That boy ain't gone cause no harm, he know the game more than the niggas I got around me," Uncle Stino says confidently.

"I ain't do it anyway," Stino proclaimed.

"Anyways, how'd they do last week?" Unc Stino asks.

"It's in the safe. They did better than the week before," Mama answered.

Stino walks to the safe, which is under the floor in mama's bedroom. He pulls out 25k and leaves 5k in the safe.

"Its 2.5k for you and the rest for the boys," Unc Stino says, returning back in the kitchen.

"All right, little, niggas I'll see y'all later!" Stino yells to the boys.

"All right, Unc!" we all yell back.

"All right, Eve, I'ma see you next week. Hit me if you need me," Stino says to Mama.

"Bye, Nigga!" Mama says.

Mama goes to here room take out one thousand dollars out the safe.

"Bobby and Michael, come here!" Mama yells my name and my twin brother's name. "Here y'all go, don't spend that shit up on no damn shoes either, Bobby," she says while handing us both five hundred dollars.

"This all we get? I need to start my own business," Bobby says.

"Shut up, boy! You lucky your uncle even helping us out. After all he do for us, you should be grateful you get that much," Mama tells Bobby.

"You right, Mama, thank you," Bobby says.

"Thank you, Mama," I say.

"Now y'all give me a kiss and gone and get y'all asses to school before the Child Protective Services be calling my phone again. And Bobby, you better take your ass to each class. You better not miss none of them, or I'ma beat yo ass for a week straight!" Mama yells as we leave her room.

"Man, this some *bullshit*, I know we racked up more than 20k for that nigga, and he only toss us 500 each, yo! That nigga cheap ass fuck," Bobby says to me, walking back to our rooms.

I smile at him because I know exactly how much we made but don't say nothing.

"Mom's got a point, he has been taken care of us since Pops died," I remind Bobby.

"*Damn*, get off that nigga's nuts," Bobby says, showing the frustration in his voice.

I push him and say, "Shut up, bitch!"

As we leave the house heading for school, we see a crowd of people around the yellow tape, which is circled around Twan's body with a white blanket over it. We drop Lil D off at school and make our way to our school. We were waiting at the bus stop because our school was further from home than Lil D.

"Man, they just had to shoot that nigga right where we play basketball at. That nigga been down there for two hours already. I hope they pick that nigga up before we get out of school, 'cause I'm trying to shoot some hoops," Bobby says.

"Bro, you ain't got no respect," I say to Bobby.

"Man, fuck that nigga, he should've never ratted on Unc," Bobby suggests.

"Nigga, you don't even know what happen," I say.

"Sooooo! What's all there you need to know? Them niggas hit worm house, that nigga Twan got caught, and he out the next week. What that tell you?"

Bobby looks at me as if he is waiting for response.

I shrug my shoulders. "I don't know," I say, not really concerned.

"*Snitch*! He a snitch!" Bobby yells out.

I shake my head and say, "I guess I mean…"

"Unc already told me he did it anyways," Bobby says.

"Nigga, you told me he winked and grinned," I say.

"Bra! Read between the bars," Bobby says with his hands up.

"Nigga, it's read between the lines dumbass," I say snickering, 'cause this nigga Bobby was a fool.

Chapter 2

Speaking on the Dead!

"What's up, Bobby?" Dave, Bobby's friend, yells from across the street.

"Nigga, wassup! You see that body by my house? They smacked that nigga," Bobby says while walking up to Dave, both of them greeting one another with a high five.

"Nah, I ain't seen it," Dave says, looking a little puzzled as him and Bobby finished crossing the street.

"Bro, you better watch who you speakin' on," a voice from the crowd at the bus stop says.

Bobby turns around hella fast and try to find out who said that. Out walks a dread-head teenager with a gang of tattoos repping south side Richmond on his arms. Don't be speaking on my cousin Twan, *nigga*!" the young dread head says as he shakes his head to move his dreads out of his face.

"Well, that nigga should've never thought it was okay to rat on my Unc, now he ain't gone get the chance to rat on nobody, nomore. For good, that's facts," Bobby says without even blinking.

"What, nigga? My cousin wasn't no rat. If anybody a rat, yo fat-ass uncle is. How you think he making all that cheese off dope? Cause he ratting on the real niggas," Dread Head shakes his head again, moving his hair back out of his face.

"Nigga, you must be on dope if you think my Unc a snitch!" yells Bobby.

"Nigga, all of Richmond know yo Unc a setup artist," Dread Head states.

"Yeah, just like he set up to have yo bitch-ass cousin hit too," Bobby says sarcastically but really serious at the same time.

The teenager lunges at bobby with a right hook and hits him in the face. I instantly react and sock the teenager in the face and knock him down. Bobby pushes me away and hops on the teenager, starts punching him in the face while holding his dreads down.

Some adults that were driving stopped their car and got out to break up the fight.

Bobby still fired up, so he pulling his pants up still yelling, "Okay, nigga, you gone see yo cousin real soon if you keep fucking with me!"

"Fuck you, nigga, don't let me catch yo ass slippin, nigga, it's fonk on site!" Teenager yells back while being pulled away.

"Yeah, yeah, yeah, nigga, you ain't gone bust a grape. I stay ready for bitches like you," Bobby say, not even trippin.

"It's all good, bro, I'ma see you around," the teenager says.

Bobby flips him off and pushes the white guy that was holding him back.

"Nigga get off of me!" Bobby yells.

"Y'all need to stop all that damn fighting," the white man says.

"Fuck you, redneck," Bobby says, snarling at the white guy.

The white guy acts as if he was gone hit Bobby, but the bus pulls up, so he shakes his head and says, "The hell with you niggers."

I grab Bobby and tell him to get on the bus. We get on the bus, and the bus driver asks what happened. Everyone who, got on the bus said the same thing, they didn't see nothing.

Me and Bobby found a seat and acted as if nothing had happened. As we arrived to school, kids were already gossiping about the fight. Asking who won, who was fighting, why did they fight, and who had the video of it. As soon as one person saw the fight, the whole school saw it. So of course Bobby and his big mouth goes around school boasting off that, saying he beat his ass. In the video it only shows Bobby on top of the guy hitting him and not how he actually got to the ground.

CHAPTER 3

BRAGGING RIGHTS

Lunch bell rings. "Hey, Michael," Mary says. Mary is Michael's girl best friend since five years of age.

"Hey, Mary," I say.

"I see Bobby got into another fight today," Mary says.

I roll my eyes. "Yeah, you can say that," I say with a smirk.

"What happened?" Mary asks.

"Bobby was running off at the mouth about Twan getting hit, and Twan lil cousin stole on Bobby, and I stole on him," I explain.

She laughs.

"Bobby has been saying that the nigga owed him money, and he been trying to find him for weeks and finally saw him and beat his ass."

"I should've known he was lying with that big as knot on his head" Mary says.

I shake my head. "Yeah, that nigga was jawsin, one of these days a nigga gone beat his ass, and I ain't gone be there to help him," I say.

"Speaking of the devil," Mary says.

"Awwww, look at the cute couple," Bobby says, smiling at Mary and me.

"Shut up, Bobby, I ain't in the mood," I say.

"Man, Mary, can you hurry up and give my brother some of that pussy? This nigga been acting like a bitch lately, maybe a good nut will do him some good," Bobby says, trying to act tough in front his friends.

"At least I ain't get punched like no bitch today," I say, looking him in his eyes.

His friends and everyone who heard me starts looking around, whispering to one another.

"Nigga, shut up, I ain't get punched like no bitch. That nigga sucker punched me when I wasn't looking," Bobby says, trying to clear the air and defend himself.

"Oh, my bad, I must've heard wrong then because I just heard he owed you some money, and you whooped his ass," I say.

Bobby looks around as everyone looks at him, waiting for a response from him.

"Fuck you, Michael. You a hating-ass nigga. Come on, y'all," Bobby says as he leaves with his friends.

I laugh. "He gone try to fight me when we go home," I say to Mary.

"I guess I should be glad I'm an only child," Mary says.

"Why you say that?" I ask.

"Because if I had a brother like yours, I'll go crazy," Mary says.

"He ain't all bad, he just talk too much and don't know when to shut up," I say. Mary looks at me and shakes her head.

Chapter 4

Them Niggas!

Lunch bell rings.

"We'll see you after school," Mary says. "All right?"

Sitting in my last class of the day, I stare out the window waiting for the bell to ring. When looking out the window, I see four black niggas in hoodies that I've never seen before. I didn't pay much attention at first, until one of them removed his hoodie, and then I recognized the dread-headed teenager from the bus stop this morning. I hop out my seat, knowing what they are here for.

"Sit down, Michael," Teacher says.

I run out of the classroom to go find Bobby, only to find out that he didn't show up to his last class and left school early.

I call his phone over and over but no answer. At the park around the corner from the school (phone buzzing over and over).

"Damn, that bitch Keisha blowing you up again," Dave says as he inhales weed smoke.

"Naw, that's my bitch-ass brother, that nigga be getting on my nerves. Damn nigga, pass that shit," Bobby says.

"Nigga, you just gave it to me, damn," Dave says.

"Nigga it's my shit so give it here," Bobby says.

"Nigga, here take yo bunk-ass weed, that shit wasn't even hitting anyway," Dave says while leaving the park.

"Yeah, you ain't say that shit 'bout the last blunt!" Bobby yells at Dave.

Bobby finishes smoking the rest of the blunt and starts to walk back to the school to catch the bus home. As Dave walks back to school, he runs into the boys in da hood. He notices one of their faces. One of them ask, "Aye lil homie, you seen that nigga Bobby around?"

"Yeah, that nigga at da park," Dave responds.

All four boys walk down to the park as Dave makes his way back to school. I run out the school front door looking to see if I see Bobby anywhere, and that's when I spot Dave. I run to him, asking have he seen Bobby "Damn, why everybody looking for that nigga? His weed is not that good," Dave says.

"Nigga, the dude Bobby fought is up here with three other niggas. I saw them outside my classroom window," I say.

"Yo! I knew I recognized that nigga from somewhere," Dave says.

"You saw them?" I ask.

"Yeah, I thought they was some customers of y'alls, so I told them he was at the park," Dave says.

"Nigga, come on!" I say.

We both run toward the park.

CHAPTER 5

CAUGHT SLIPPIN'

Bobby still walking back to the school, texting Keisha with his head down.

"I told you, nigga, I bet not catch you slippin," a familiar voice out of the four boys says to Bobby. Bobby looks up to notice he surrounded by four niggas in black hoodies. The teenager with dreads removes his hood.

"What's all that shit you was talking about my cousin Twan?" the teenager says.

"That the nigga is a sni—" Right before he could get the snitch word out of his mouth, one of the hooded dudes sucker punches him in the mouth from the side. He drops to his knees, leaving him leaking with blood pouring from his mouth. As he's on his knees, he sees a big rock and picks it up and uppercuts the guy who punches him and knocks him out. Bobby tries to run, but the two other hooded men catches him, and each holds one of his arms. Me and Dave turn the corner just to witness the two hooded men holding bobby. "Y'all better let my brother go!" I yell from the corner as me and Dave continued running their way.

The teenager notices who I was and grinned.

"Looks like big brother trying to come be captain save a bitch again," he says.

Bobby spits blood at the teenager's face.

"Fuck you, bitch," Bobby says leaking blood.

17

The teenager wipes his face and pulls out a .45 Glock.

"Tell my cousin Twan, wassup!" *BANG! BANG! BANG!* He shoots Bobby three times in the chest, and the hooded men run off.

"Noooooooooooooo!" I yell out. Me and Dave witnessing the whole thing, running toward Bobby. As I get to Bobby I cradle him in my arms, trying to stop the blood from coming out his chest.

"Bro! You gone be okay," I tell Bobby as he coughing up blood. Dave tries to run after the hooded men, but they hop in a four-door bucket and got away.

"Somebody help!" I yell as Dave returns just to see that Bobby has passed away.

"Dave, call the ambulance!" I yell at him.

"Look what them niggas did to my brother," I say, tears coming down my face as I hold Bobby closer.

CHAPTER 6

CALL 911!

Dave gets on the phone to call 911.

"911, what's your emergency?" the 911 dispatch says.

"Yeah, man, my nigga Bobby got shot," Dave says.

"Okay, what's your name and your number?" the 911 dispatch says. "Bitch, why you got to know my name if I'm not the one shot?" Dave says, irritated.

"Dave, stop playing, man, and get my brother some help," I say.

"Nigga this bitch trying to know all my info instead of your brother's," Dave says.

"Dave!" I yell.

"All right, damn my name Dave Dicksworth, my number is—" Dave says but gets interrupted by dispatch.

"Excuse me, can you repeat your name one more time?" the 911 dispatch says.

"Dave Dicksworth," Dave says.

The dispatch starts busting out laughing.

"Bitch, are you seriously laughing at my name when I'm calling to tell you my nigga got shot? Y'all niggas ain't shit. Can your dumbass please send an ambulance to South 35 and cutting near the park?" Dave yells into the phone and hangs up.

Chapter 7

Why My Brother?

"Come on, man, stay in there. You gone make it," I tell Bobby, rocking his dead body back and forth. All of a sudden, a crowd of people surround us because of hearing the gunshots.

"Back up, y'all, give us some space!" Dave yells out to everyone.

He looks at Bobby, knowing he's dead but not wanting to tell me. Whispering goes around among the crowd.

"Damn, they smacked Lil Bobby someone says in the crowd. I cradle his body closer and closer knowing deep down my brother is gone, but I can't let him go.

"Bobby, wake up, bro, come on we got to go home," I say.

Mary makes her way through the crowd, hearing that Bobby got shot and notices me holding his body. She comes to my side to try to comfort me.

"Michael, are you hurt?" Mary asks.

"They killed my brother," I say to her, looking at Bobby in his eyes.

"Who did?" Mary asks.

"That nigga from this morning, that Bobby fought," I say.

"So who is the guy on the floor lying down? Is he dead too?" Mary asks and points to the hooded man Bobby had knocked out with the rock.

"It was him, the dread head from this morning and two other niggas," I say while placing Bobby's body down.

I get up and walk over to the hooded man body and slapped this shit out of him.

WHAAAPP!

"Wake up, you bitch-ass nigga," I say to the hooded man as I smack him across the face.

"Ouuuuhh! Whatchu do that for?" the hooded dude says, awakening from the slap.

"Nigga, you killed my brother," I say as I punch him right in the nose. Pow! He covers his face because of the blood coming from his mouth and nose.

"Nigga, I didn't have yo brother killed," he mumbles in his hands.

"Nigga, what you say?" I ask as I cock my fist back, ready to punch again. He lowers his hands and says, "Nigga, I didn't have nothing to do with yo brother gettin' killed we was told to only scare the little nigga."

"What's yo name, bitch-ass nigga?" Dave asks. Wiping the blood from his mouth, he says, "My name's Jordan."

"Wait a minute, ain't you Twan little brother? From the south side?" Dave asks.

"Yeah, that's me, my cousin Adam told me yo brother was down talking bad about my brother and hollering about how my cousin owed yo brother some money, but we was told to only hurt him not kill him," Hooded man says.

"What you mean you was told to hurt him? And wait a min how y'all know what fucking school we went to anyway?" I say, a bit puzzled.

"Nigga, our OG told us everything 'bout yo little brother. Twan was his number-one runner, and we don't let nobody speak on the dead," the hooded man says right before spitting out a gang of blood toward Bobby's body.

"Nigga!" I jump on the hooded man and start giving him blows to the head.

"Hey, get off him!" a man says, coming out of the crowd that's just watching and recording, and he tries to pull me off of the hooded man.

"Get the fuck off me, bruh. He killed my brother!" I yell at the man, trying to escape his grasp.

"Nigga, I told you we wasn't posed to kill him! That nigga Adam must've did it on his own because my OG Nits-O would never put a hit out on a kid," the hooded man says as he holds his head.

"Nigga, *fuck you*. Adam, Nits-O, and them other niggas too! Y'all gone get it just watch," I say, trying to still escape the man's arms.

Chapter 8

Help Has Arrived

Blurrrr! Bluurr! Fire truck sirens goes off arriving forty-five minutes later with two cop cars right behind it.

"Y'all bitches hurry up!" Dave yells to them as they exit their vehicles.

The man lets me go when he sees the officers. I immediately run toward the hooded man to punch him in the face, he drops again. The cops run over to grab and detain me.

"What the hell's going on here?" the white cop says, tipping his hat back, noticing Bobby's body on the ground.

"That nigga *killed* my brother!" I yell out.

"Nigga, stop saying that, we only was posed to hurt him not kill him!" the hooded man yells back.

I try to break away from the cop.

"Michael, calm yo ass down!" the black cop says, holding me."

I instantly look back. "How you know my name?" I ask.

"I know all about you and your brothers, y'all David boys," the black cop says.

"Leave my dad name out yo mouth," I say.

"Nigga, hush I knew yo dad before you was even thought of," the black cop says.

I roll my eyes and tell him to let me go.

"Are you going to act right, or do I need to place you under arrest?" the black cop says.

23

"Arrest for what? He ain't do nothing!" Dave yells out.

"Little nigger, you want to go too?" the white cop says.

"Naw, I'm good," Dave says.

"You fat bitch," Dave mumbles under his breath while walking toward the crowd.

"What you say, you little fuck?" the white cop says.

"I ain't say nothing," Dave says while smiling. "Yeah, I thought, so."

"So who wants to tell me what the hell happened here?" the white cop says.

"Man, they killed my brother!" I say.

"Who are they?" the black cop says.

"Him and some other niggas my brother had a beef with this morning," I say, pointing at the hooded man.

"Damn, snitch!" the hooded man says.

"Bitch-ass nigga, you lucky they even here, or I'll still be whooping yo ass!" I yell at him, trying get to him.

"All right, Michael. That's it. You're going in the car till we get things in control," the black cop says.

"Man, I ain't even do nothing," I say.

"Yeah, I know you didn't, I'm just trying to keep it that way," the black cop says.

"Nigga, don't act like you care 'bout me. My uncle told me about you, Officer Kane," I say to him as I'm being escorted to the cop car.

"You know he's not really your uncle, right? He just using y'all kids to move his product," Officer Kane states.

"What product?" I say. Officer Kane starts to chuckle while putting me in the cop car.

"Man, why y'all arresting Michael? He the one who killed bobby," Dave says, irritated.

"Young man, one more word out of you, and you gone be joining Mr. Michael," black cop officer Kane says.

Dave looks at the ground and shuts up.

"Get on your feet and place your hands behind your back," the white cop says to the hooded man.

"Call it in Kane," the white cop says.

"Dispatch, do you copy?" Kane begins to speak into the radio.

"Go ahead, Officer Kane," dispatch says.

"Bitch, why you didn't ask for his name?" Dave yells out so dispatch can hear. Kane covers the radio and looks at Dave and tells him to shut up.

"What kind of car was the suspects in?" Kane asks.

"Oh, now you want me to talk?" Dave says.

"Boy, if you…" Kane starts talking but quickly stops in his tracks, remembering he was still on radio.

"What car were they in?" Kane says with force.

"They was in a blue bucket," Dave says.

The white cop laughs. "Of course, they are," he says.

"What kind of bucket?" Kane asks.

"A four-door Camry, probably like a '98 or '96," Dave says.

"Dispatch, can you put out an APB on a blue Toyota Camry with three suspects fleeing the scene of a homicide. A teenager has been shot multiple times and is deceased," Kane says.

"How'd you know how many guys was here?" Dave asks.

"Michael told me when I walked him over to the car," Kane lies.

"Let's go, young man, you're under arrest for murder," the white cop says to the hooded man.

Bluurrrp! Bluurrp! Bluurrpp!

"Finally, backup has arrived," the white cop says as he escorts the hooded man to the backup cop cars.

"All right, back up! back up, people!" the backup cop says as he begins to try to get the crowed under control.

"What the he'll going on here, Gable?" the backup cop says to the white cop.

"One of the Stino boys got killed. Here's one of the four suspects now," Gable says.

"Oh shit, what happened? Does Stino know yet?" the backup cop says, taking his hat off and scratching his head.

"I don't know if he knows yet. I don't even know anything yet, but I believe this young man does."

"Get in there," Gable says, shoving the hooded man in the back of the cop car. "This is bad. You know that, right?" the backup cop says.

"What do you mean?" Gable says.

"That's little Bobby over there, isn't it?" Backup asks.

"Yeah, you know him?" Gable asks.

"Everyone knows lil Bobby and Michael, they are little David's boy," Backup cop says.

"Who the fuck is David? I heard Kane mention him earlier," Gable says.

"David was Stino's brother. They ran Richmond together until David got killed and Stino took over and took care of David's boys." Backup cop says.

"Where are you from, rookie?" Backup cop asks.

"Chicago," Gable says.

"You're a long way from home, rookie. Keep your head down and listen to Kane, he'll keep you alive. He's been on the force ten years now, and he's seen a lot and knows a lot," Backup cop informs Gable.

"I guess I'm not too far from home," Gable says.

"What you mean by that?" Backup cop says.

"I left Chicago because of all the senseless killings surrounding bad neighborhoods, and it's the same here as it is there," Gable says.

Sirens blaring in the background.

"Finally the ambulance has come," Gable says.

"Hey, guys, over here," Gable directs them to the cop car to take a look at the hooded man face and points to Bobby's dead body. An EMT puts the hooded man on a gurney, handcuffed, and escorts him to the ambulance.

"All right, let's back these people up and set up some tape and get ready for the coroner," Backup cop says.

"Good thinking, Joshua," Kane says.

The ambulance pulls off.

CHAPTER 9

MY BABY, MY BABY!

Tires pull up screeching from a Jaguar.

"I know that ain't my baby," Eve says, running out of the passenger side toward Bobby's body.

"Oh my god, they killed my baby, Eve," he says, realizing it's Bobby's body.

Stino exits the driver's side of the car, walking over to Bobby's body.

"Who the fuck did this shit?" Stino yells as he is realizing it's Bobby.

"*Ooohhhhhh!* Lord Jesus, why, my baby, my sweet, sweet baby. Why not me, Lord? Take me, Lord!" Eve yells to the sky.

"Why you take my baby away from me, Lord? *Ooohh!*"

"No! No! No! No! No! Stino, look what they did to my baby!" Eve cries.

"This is all your fault, you killed my baby," Eve says.

"Bitch, shut up! How I killed your baby when I was with you the whole time? We gone fasho find the niggas that did this shit and they gone pay, believe that," Stino says, turning around and noticing me in the back of a cop car with Kane standing right next to it.

"Why the fuck my nephew in that car?" Stino asks while walking over to the car.

"He was trying to beat the living crap out of one of the suspects, so I placed his ass in there to cool off," Kane says answers.

"Bitch, nigga, let him out, he ain't do shit but loose a brother, and you gone arrest him for that," Stino says, getting in Kane's face.

"Mr. Stino, I would advise you to back the fuck up before I replace him with your ass," Kane says.

Stino backs up.

"Thought so," Kane says while letting me exit the cop car and runs to Stino's arms.

"They killed him, Uncle," I say.

"I know, Mike, it's gone be all right. We gone get them niggas, don't worry," Stino says.

"*Ooohh* lord. Why? My baby!" Eve screams.

"Michael, where were you? Why you just let them kill your brother like this? Your daddy left you in charge of us to protect us, and you couldn't even do that now. Look at my baby!" Eve yells.

"Eve, you need to shut up and stop trying to blame everybody but yourself. You the real reason he dead," Stino says.

"What the fuck you say?" Eve asks, running toward Stino, trying to hit him. "Move, bitch, before I really hurt you," Stino says.

"Fuck you, Stino. If Bobby wasn't running for you, he wouldn't be dead right now," Eve says.

"Bitch, you better shut up before I shut you up," Stino says.

"Is there a problem over here?" Kane asks.

"Naw we good," Stino says.

"Naw we ain't good. My son is fucking dead right here on the sidewalk just laid out. Why y'all ain't covering my boy body?"

"What the hell y'all gone do 'bout who killed my baby?" Eve asks.

"Ma'am, we have a suspect in custody now and we're looking for the rest now. They escaped in a blue four-door Camry," Kane says, trying to reassure Eve.

"The rest, how many was there?" Stino asks.

"That's information that can't be disclosed at this moment, Mr. Stino," Kane says.

"WTF you mean it can't be disclosed? That's my nephew right there, dead," Stino says.

"I understand that, sir, but the police have this under control, so there's no need to do anything that you might regret," Kane explains with a serious face.

"No offense, Officer, but we both know that y'all would never catch the killers just like y'all never found my brother David killer," Stino says back.

"But best believe, these niggas gone get it each and every last one of them," Stino says.

"You know I can arrest you for threats on a person life?" Kane says.

"Oh yeah? What's the charges on a promise on a person life?" Stino replies.

"How about life with your old friend Peter?" Kane says, turning his Back as he sees the coroner arrive.

Stino looked as if he saw a ghost as soon as he hears that name when I looked at his face.

"All right, guys, the victim's over there." Joshua points to Bobby's body.

Chapter 10

Don't Snitch!

"Come on, y'all have to let the coroner do they job this is a crime scene now," Kane says, walking back to escort us behind the yellow tape.

"Michael, can you come with us down to the station so we can ask you a few questions?" Kane asks.

"For what?" Stino asks.

"For the murder of his brother, of course, unless he has something else he has to hide," Kane says.

"Why we can't take him?" Stino asks.

"No one said you couldn't," Mr. Stino Kane says.

"Okay, then we will meet you guys down there," Stino says.

"No need, we have a police escort for you, Mr. Stino," Kane suggests.

"Why y'all need all that for? We ain't nobody special," Stino says.

"Just to make sure y'all get to the police station safely, that's it," Kane says.

"Yeah, okay," Stino says.

"Come on y'all," Stino demands.

"No, I'm not leaving till they pick my baby up," Eve says with a face filled with tears.

"Eve, they need us at the police station," Stino says.

"Actually, we only need Michael to come answer a few questions, we don't need you guys there," Kane says.

"Then take him, I'm not leaving Bobby's side," Eve says.

"Hold on, let me talk to you Michael," Stino tells me as he pulls me to the side.

"Mike, you know not to tell these pigs shit, right? You know we gone handle this on our own?" Stino whispers to me.

"You promise, Unc?" I ask.

"I had my niggas looking for these fools as soon as I heard the shit happened," Stino says.

"How you find out, Unc?" I ask.

"You know how these streets be talking, and everybody know y'all my boys, so you know I'm the first to hear about anything that happens to y'all," Stino says.

"Okay, Unc. I'm sorry I wasn't there to help Bobby. I really tried," I say.

"Son, it's okay. I know it's not your fault, but tell me this. Do you want to be there to get justice for your brother?" Stino asks with a serious face.

"You know I do, Unc," I say.

"Well, tell these pigs nothing and call me as soon as they about to let you go, and I'll be waiting for you right outside that police station," Stino says.

"Why won't you just come with me, Unc?"

"Because I'm going to try to find the niggas that did this shit," Stino says.

"OK, Unc, I got you," I say.

"I love you, son, and best believe we gone get revenge for Bobby," Stino says.

"I love you to, Unc," I say back, giving him a hug.

"All right, Mr. Kane, I'm ready," I say.

"This way, Michael, you can go in the car with Mr. Dave," Kane says.

"Why y'all arresting Dave?" I ask.

"We are not arresting him, we are bringing him in for questioning also," Kane says, looking back at Stino.

"All right! In you go," Gable says.

"Wassup, Mike, you good?" Dave asks as I get in the back of the cop car with him.

"Yeah, bro, I'm good," I replied.

"Aye, bro, you know you can't say shit to the police," I say.

"About what?" Dave asks.

"Nigga about the niggas that killed Bobby and what we saw," I say.

"Who killed Bobby, and what you mean what we saw?" Dave says with a smirk.

I look at him, noticing he knows what I'm talking about.

"Nigga, I know wassup, my dad in jail because some niggas snitched on him. Well, at least that what Mom tells me," Dave says.

"All right, bro, good looking cause my Unc gone find these niggas," I say.

"What niggas y'all talking about?" Gable says, entering the cop car from the passenger side.

"None, we was talking about our slaved ancestors. You know the ones yo great-grandparents used to own?" Dave says with a smart remark.

"Little nigga, you don't none about me or my ancestors, so I'll advise you to shut the fuck up before this questioning turns into reading you your rights," Gable says as he turns around angrily.

"I must've hit a button there." Dave smirks.

"What's going on in here?" Kane asks, entering the cop car.

"Nothing," Gable says, turning back around.

"All right, boys, we gone go down here and just ask you guys a few questions, then we will return you back to your parents," Kane says, pulling off in the car.

Dave and me look at each other in silence, still in a bit of disbelief.

"Who's the guy, Peter, you were talking about? I saw Mr. Stino look as if he saw a ghost."

"A big-time drug dealer from back in the day that used to run the streets. He got busted in a sting operation. He been locked up for ten years now. It's actually the same night Mr. David died," Kane says, looking in the review mirror at me. I look at him back.

"Shut up. You don't know nothing about my dad," I say.

"Son, I've known your dad since we were in high school. I know him a lot more than you do," Kane says.

"Don't call me your son," I say.

"Look, I know you're going through a lot right now, losing your brother and all, but I don't know what you expected living the life you and your brothers are living," Kane says.

"And what life is that, Officer?" I say.

"The life Mr. Stino have you children living. Running his drugs around Richmond," Kane says bluntly, staring at me in the review mirror. Making sure they made eye contact.

"I don't know what you are talking about, officer. My uncle Stino is a businessman, he has plenty businesses he owns," I say.

"Ahahaha. Oh trust me we know all about the businesses he owns and how he's washing his dirty money through each and every one of those establishments. That's the reason we can't find anything on him, but trust me we will. He will eventually slip up, and that's where I'm going to bust his ass for the criminal he is," Kane says.

"I ain't got nothing else to say," I say.

"It's just sad to see you kids getting killed over a few bucks. Mr. Stino should be ashamed of his self to even call you guys his nephews," Kane says as he grips the steering wheel tight. Gable turns and notices that Kane is really emotional over talking about the situation. I sit quietly, letting everything the officer said sink in. Dave nudges me. "You good, bro?" Dave whispers.

"Yeah, bro. That nigga ain't affecting me," I say, turning my head toward the window.

Chapter 11

Police Statement

"All right, boys, here we are," Kane says. We arrive to the police station, and Officer Kane lets me out, and Officer Gable lets Dave out.

"All right, I'll take Dave, and you take Michael to the interrogation room," Kane demands.

"Why don't you just take Michael since you have him, and I'll take Dave?" Gable says. "Because I know his father, I'm not allowed to interview a person with any personal relationship with my personal life," Kane says.

"Wow you guys got some weird laws in Cali," Gable says trying to make a joke.

"Are you questioning me, rookie?" Kane asks.

"Nope. No, sir," Gable answers.

"Good, I would hate to have to replace you because I was just starting to like you," Kane says laughing while switching me for Dave.

"No need for that, sir," Gable says with a smirk on his face but feeling that Kane is hiding something.

"All right you can take Michael to room 5 and interview him there," Kane says as we walk into the police station.

"Okay, sir," Gable says.

Back in the interview room.

"All right, Mr. Dicksworth, what can you tell me about the killing of little Bobby?" Kane asks.

"First off, the name is Dave, and second I want my lawyer," Dave announces.

"Son, you're not even under arrest, there's no need for you to even have a lawyer present. Your just simply here to answer a few questions about your supposed friend who just got killed right in front of your eyes," Kane says.

"You must got a lot of kids, you call a lot of niggas your son?"

"Or are you from the Bronx because I got a cousin from New York and that nigga be calling me son when I'm older than him," Dave says, smiling.

"Do you think this is a game, little nigger? Your friend just got killed, and yo punk ass in here making jokes, some friend you are," Kane says, slamming his hands on the table as he stands up heading for the door as if he done talking to Dave.

"Wait!" Dave says. "All right I saw who killed Bobby, but I ain't no rat," Dave says.

"No one said you are, son," Kane says.

"A'ite, look, if you don't want me to start collecting child support for all the years you missed in my life, I suggest you stop calling me son, or else I ain't talking," Dave says.

"Okay, I'm listening," Kane says as he sits back down. "Well, I don't know the nigga name, but Bobby was telling me that nigga had owed him some money and Bobby caught that nigga slipping this morning at the bus stop and got on that nigga," Dave explains.

"Why did the guy owe him money?" Kane asks.

"I don't know all that, man, he just said he owed him money," Dave answers.

"Okay, so how'd Bobby end up dead at the park?" Kane proceeds to try and get a couple more answers to his questions.

"I guess the dude from earlier didn't like how Bobby got at him at the bus stop and went to go get the other guys," Dave says.

"And there were three other guys you said, right?" Kane says.

"No, I didn't say how many guys there was," Dave says, remembering Kane said Michael told him it was three other guys."

"Oh, okay, I'm sorry. I must've heard wrong. How many would you say were there at the scene?" Kane continues to keep pushing questions.

"I don't know, I saw at least three dudes, but it was all happening so fast, I could only see Bobby getting shot and his body hitting the ground," Dave says, starting to cry.

"It's gone be okay, son," Kane says.

"Nigga!" Dave says, wiping his tears quickly after hearing him say *son*.

"Sorry. But did you get a good look at the shooter?" Kane asks.

"Naw, he had his hoodie on, but I did see dreads hanging out of his hoodie, though. And the guy Bobby said he fought had dreads," Dave says.

"So you didn't come in contact with any of the suspects at any time?" Kane asks.

Dave looks nervously because he was the one who told the suspects where Bobby would be. "No, dad, I didn't," Dave finally answers.

"All right, lil smartass, you're free to go we will contact you if we have more questions," Kane says.

"How are you feeling, Mr. Michael?" Gable asks, trying to break the ice.

"Let me ask you something. Do you have any siblings?" I ask.

"Yes, I do. Four older brothers and one older sister," Gable answers.

"Are any of them dead?" I ask.

"No, they are not," Gable answers. "Then you wouldn't know how I'm feeling right now. They killed my brother and y'all over asking me and Dave questions when y'all need to get out there and try to find my brother killer," I say.

"That's why we brung you guys in to get more information about the suspects," Gable says.

"Man I don't know nothing," I say.

"Well, Officer Kane tells me you told him that there was three other suspects other than the killer," Gable says.

"What? I never told him that. I don't know how many there was. I just saw one guy shoot my brother point-blank in his face while some other niggas was holding him," I say.

"So you didn't tell Officer Kane that you saw all four suspects?" Gable says.

"No. Why do you keep saying that? All he was talking about is how he know my pops and some bullshit about my uncle," I say.

"And your uncle is Mr. Stino, is that correct?" Gable asks.

"Yes, he is, after my dad died he been there for us ever since," I say.

"So you think that just because you guys sell his dope on street corners, he is taking care of y'all? He is using y'all little kids, and unfortunately your brother was casualty," Gable says.

"Shut up. You act like you know our life. You don't know what struggle is out here, and now I'm the one that got to bury my brother. Fuck you, pig! I ain't saying shit else. You don't know what it feels like to bury my dad and now my brother," I say.

"You right, I don't know what that feels like, but I do know what hurt is because I lost my six-year-old daughter to a stray bullet at a park she was playing at in Chicago. She was innocent, just like you kids were probably before you guys started selling drugs, and it's a shame to see such great youth go to waste," Gable says as he stands up, gathering his things to leave.

"Did you ever catch your daughter killer?" I ask as he opens the door. He stops and put his head down.

"Yes, I did," Gable says as he turns around.

"Did you kill him?" I ask.

He closes the door and says, "No he's rotting in prison for being the criminal that he is."

"Why didn't you kill him? I swear once I catch the nigga that killed my brother I'm going to blow his dreads back," I say.

"You know that's a threat, but I know you going through a lot right now, so I'll let it slide. But where would killing him get you?" Gable asks.

"It'll get justice for Bobby, that's what it will do," I say.

"So would turning him in and letting the system serve justice," Gable says.

"No offense, but the system haven't done my family no good y'all still haven't even found my dad killer, so how y'all supposed to find my brothers?" I say.

"I don't know anything about your father's case, but I can promise you that we will find the killer and get justice for your brother," Gable tries to assure me.

"Don't make no promises you can't keep, officer. I promised my family I would be the man of the house and take care of them, and look how my brother ended up," I say, looking him dead in his eyes, so he can know for sure how serious I am.

"How old are you, son?" Gable asks.

"Sixteen," I tell him.

"Son, you still have so much more in store for you if you only make the right decisions. From now on, you can be that man your family needs you to be. If you ever need anything or to talk to me, here's my personal cell phone number. You can use it at any time you need me," Gable lets me know while writing his phone number on a piece of paper.

"Thank you, Officer Gable," I say.

CHAPTER 12

A DRUNK WOMAN
TELLS NO LIES

"No problem, son, let's get you guys back to your parents," Gable says.

"Okay," I say as we leave the room.

"What happened down at the police station?" Stino asks as soon as I walk through the door after the police dropped me off.

"Nothing, the officer tried to get me talking about our family and you," I tell him.

"Man, I knew that Officer Kane was a bitch!"

"What did you say to him?" Stino asks.

"I talked to Officer Gable, not Kane, he talked to Dave, and they had us in separate rooms," I inform him.

"So what you say to him, nigga?" Stino asks, a bit antsy.

"I didn't say shit. They asked if I knew who killed Bobby, and I said I didn't get a clear view of his face or how many was there," I say.

"What about yo homeboy Dave, what he say?" Stino asks.

"That's Bobby's homeboy, not mine and I don't know. I didn't talk to him since they separated and had us in different rooms," I say.

"Well, where that nigga stay at?" Stino asks.

"I don't know," I say.

"A'ite, lil nigga, you did good," Stino compliments.

"So what we gone do about these niggas that killed Bobby?" I ask.

"Don't worry I'm gone take care of this. I'ma make show them niggas pay," Stino says.

"No! That was my brother. I want to be the one take care of them niggas," I say.

"Lil Nigga, I ain't talking about beating no niggas up with yo hands. They took your brother, and I told yo daddy that I had y'all, and I failed him so we taken life's for a life youngsta," Stino says.

"Yeah, I know I'm ready for it I'm ready for my first body," I say, anxious.

"Lil nigga you sure about that? Ain't no coming back from you shooting your first shot," Stino says.

"Ain't no coming back for my brother either, I'm ready," I say.

"You ready for what?" Eve comes in with a bottle of Hennessey in her hand.

"Nothing, Eve, take yo ass back to yo room," Stino says.

"Nigga, you ain't my damn daddy, and this my damn house. Do you pay the rent here?" Eve says drunkenly.

"Matter of fact I do," Stino says.

"Oh, well good for you, you still ain't my damn daddy," Eve says.

"Woman, you need to go to yo room," Stino says again.

"No, I need to know why this bitch nigga let them niggas kill my boy," Eve says, pointing at me.

"Eve, Mike ain't have nothing to do with Bobby killing, so stop blaming him," Stino says.

"Blah blah blah, motherfuckin' blah. You sound like a bitch," Eve says, taking another sip out her bottle.

"A'ite, I see you too damn drunk to talk to, so I'ma go before things get out of hand here. I'ma try to go find out some information on what happened to Bobby," Stino says.

"Same old Stino, always running away just like you used to do," Eve says.

"Shut up, bitch, you don't know what you talking about," Stino says, putting on his jacket.

"Fuck you, nigga, I'm glad I never had a baby with you," Eve says, taking another sip.

"Bitch, go to yo room now because you starting to sound and look stupid," Stino says.

"Call me another bitch," Eve says.

"Bitch, go now!" Stino yells.

"That's a good boy, I knew you could listen," Eve says taking another sip.

Stino raises his hand as if he was about to hit her but sees me and retracts his hand.

"Michael, you want me to drop you off somewhere so you ain't got to deal with this crazy woman?" Stino says.

"Naw, I'm good, Uncle. I'ma just go lock myself in the room," I say.

"Like a little bitch." Eve snickers.

Stino looks at Eve, disgusted like he wanted to continue to slap her.

"Call me if you need me, little nigga, and I'ma let you know when I need you for that mission," Stino says.

"A'ite, Uncle, I love you," I say.

"Love you too, boy."

"Bye, bitch," Stino says.

"Bye, nigga," Eve says, taking another sip.

"You know you a little bitch, right?" Eve says.

"Mom, your drunk right now, you don't mean what you saying," I say.

She takes a sip. "Nigga, don't tell me how the fuck I'm feeling or how the fuck to talk. I'm yo damn Mama, I brung you in this world to take care of me, and you can't even take care of your little brother."

"Huh, sounds like a bitch to me," Eve says as she take another sip.

"Fuck you, bitch, you ain't did shit for us our whole life but fuck on Uncle Stino, so he could keep us around. If it wasn't for your dick-sucking skills we probably would've been better off in the fucking system then staying here with your drunk ass," I lash out and say.

"Nigga, what the fuck you say?" Eve says as she spits out her liquor.

"I didn't stutter, my brother and my dad would've been alive if you wasn't such a drunk bitch all the time," I say.

"You keep your father out of this, you barely even knew him so shut the fuck up, and go to your room bitch-ass nigga," Eve says, taking another sip.

"You know what? I'm kind of jealous of Bobby and Pops right now because they left me and Lil Donny here with your nonparenting ass," I say.

"Boy, ain't nobody listening to you. Go to your fucking room before I bust this bottle over yo head," Eve says.

"Where my brother at anyway?" I ask.

"You dumb fuck, didn't you just let him get shot in the face? Where the fuck you think he at?" Eve says, taking another sip.

"I'm talking about Lil Donny," I say.

"Oh, how I'm posed to know you and Bobby are the ones who pick him up from school every day? Why y'all ain't do it today?" Eve says.

"So you mean to tell me Lil Donny doesn't even know about Bobby?" I ask.

"What happened to Bobby?" Eve asks, taking another sip.

"Oh my god, I swear bitch the day will come when ain't none of us gone be here and yo dick-sucking skills gonna get old and uncle Stino gone get tired of your ass and leave yo ass in the gutter where you belong."

"Now I'm gonna go get my little Brother and make sure he good because you damn sure don't care about none of us."

"If it's not making you no money in any way," I say as I go to my room.

"Fuck you, little nigga, you think you know what I go through? You don't know shit," Eve says as she throws the bottle my way and it hits the wall. I duck, knowing the bottle hit the wall ten feet away from me.

"I swear I wish my dad was alive and you was dead," I say.

"Well, I wish Bobby was here and yo ass was out there on the fucking ground," Eve says.

I stare at her with coldhearted eyes after hearing those words.

"Oh yeah, bitch, I knew you loved him more than me and now you stuck with me. So what now? Are you going to show me the love that you never gave me, or am I just a meal ticket to you?" I say, with tears coming down my eyes.

Eve walks into the kitchen to grab another bottle and pours her another glass and takes a sip. "That depends on if you made any money today, she says.

"And if I didn't?" I reply.

"Then you need to go out there and make me my money," Eve says.

"Thanks for letting me know where we stand at, Mom, I thought all this time that you hated me because I didn't want this life. But now I see that you hate me because I'm me and now that I know that money is all you want from me, that's all we have to speak about from now on. Actually, you know what? I don't have to even go through yo drunk ass. I can go straight to my uncle Stino and cut yo middle drunk ass out the picture," I say.

"Boy, don't you try to fuck with my money. With yo brother gone you have to step it up a bit more, so hush all that nonsense up and go get that money for us," Eve says.

"Naw, Mama. You will not use me or my brothers as pawns in your life games. I'm gone find out who killed my brother and take care of that nigga on my own. All this time I thought it was I who needed you but I see it's the other way around, it's you who need me," I say.

"Michael, you can't leave, you are supposed to take care of this family. You told me you will never leave me or your brothers. You told me you would protect us, and now you want to leave because you let Bobby get killed?" Eve says.

"Bitch, I didn't get him killed, you did and you need to stop placing blame on everybody else like my Uncle Stino said earlier," I say, packing some clothes up, about to leave.

"If you really knew your Uncle Stino, you probably wouldn't look at that bitch nigga like your daddy," Eve says.

"Don't you try to bad talk my Uncle Stino, he's the only reason this family is eating how we eating. See now you trying to blame my Unc for Bobby getting killed," I say.

"Nigga, go keep following that nigga and end up just like yo daddy and Bobby. Just come back here with that money or don't come back at all," Eve says.

"Yeah okay," I say as I leave slamming the door.

Chapter 13

Bearer of Bad News

"Hello, Michael, running a little late today I see," Mr. Peters says, which is Lil Donny schoolteacher.

"Yeah, I know we having some family problems today," I say.

"Is everything okay? Do you need to talk about it?" Mr. Peters offers.

"No, there's nothing you can do to bring my brother back," I say.

"Did bobby finally go to jail? I told him when I was teaching him when y'all was little Donny's age that he would end up in jail or dead," Mr. Peters says.

"Well, bitch, you got yo wish with your hating ass," I say.

"Excuse me, young man, what did you just say?" Mr. Peters asks.

"My brother is dead!" I yell, wiping tears away from my face.

"Oh my! I'm so sorry to hear that what happened?" Mr. Peters asks.

"He died. That's all you need to know. Where's Donny?" I ask.

"He is still in the playground. Where is your mother?" the teacher asks.

"Mr. Peters, you know damn well where she at. Home getting drunk and feeling sorry for herself," I say, walking out the classroom to the playground.

"Why isn't she here to pick up Donny at this time you shouldn't be the one to pick him up?" Mr. Peters says.

"Well, if I didn't come get him then nobody would've came," I say.

"Well, I'm giving her a call right now. I don't think he should be leaving with you in this mind state," Mr. Peter says.

"Nigga, don't act like you care about our family. We all know you can't stand us because Bobby stole your car and wrecked it when he was here. Lil Donny tells us how you treat him here, and you lucky we haven't reported yo ass to the police," I say.

"Look, you little piece of shit, I was feeling bad for your disrespectful-ass family, but now all y'all can go to hell. Go get that nigga and get the hell out of my class!" Mr. Peters yells.

"Yeah, that's the Mr. Peters I remember, the same jackass who was fucking in the teacher's bathroom two weeks ago after school," I say with a smirk.

"What the hell you just say?" Mr. Peters asks.

"Oh, nothing, I'm gone get my brother and we gone leave. Good luck trying to get in contact with that crazy bitch I call Mom," I say.

"All of y'all family is fucking crazy, get the hell out" Mr. Peters says. I exit the door to the playground and yell out for Donny to let him know I'm here.

"What's up, bro! Where's Bobby at?" Donny asks. I put my head down in silence for a few seconds.

"Man bro, Bobby gone," I say.

"What that nigga ran away again, you know he probably at Dave house," Donny says, laughing.

"Naw Bro, Bobby is…," I say and start crying.

"Nigga, what you crying for?" Donny asks.

"Bobby dead, Donny!" I yell out.

"What you mean he dead?" Donny says.

"He got shot at the school," I tell him.

"Who did it?" Donny asks.

"Some niggas he got into it with this morning," I say.

"Man! What the fuck! You lying, y'all better not be trying to play a trick on me. I'm gone tell Mama," Donny says.

"Nigga, I'm not lying, Bobby really is gone I saw him die right in front of my face," I say, trying to make him see I was serious.

"Nigga and you ain't do shit to stop it? You just let them kill him?" Donny says.

"Nigga, don't get at me like that. You know damn well I tried my best to save him, but I was too late," I say wiping my tears away.

"Do Unc know? Do Mom know? What we gonna do, bro?" Donny says, asking hella questions at once.

"Yeah, they all know we trying to find them niggas now. Don't worry, we gone get them niggas for killing Bobby," I say.

"Bro. So he really gone?" Donny asks.

"Yes, bro, he gone" I say as I stand face-to-face with Donny.

Donny breaks down crying, and I start crying again. I grabbed him and hugged him.

"I know, bro, it hurts but just know I'ma always be here for you no matter what," I say.

CHAPTER 14

NIGGAS AIN'T SHIT!

Ring! Ring! Ring! My phone rings.

"Hello," I say, wiping my face of full tears.

"What up, nigga. You good?" Dave says.

"Naw, bro, I just had to tell Donny 'bout Lil Bobby. This shit weak, bro," I say in an angry voice.

"Well, bro, my nigga just called me telling me where them niggas at who killed Bobby," Dave announces.

"Where they at? Who did it, bro?" I say.

"Them niggas in Crescent Park. You remember those niggas Isaiah and Sean?" Dave asks.

"Yeah, what about them?" I say.

"My patna said he was shooting dice with them, and they was talking about a nigga Bobby and how they had that nigga begging for his life and hella other shit," Dave says.

"What nigga you talking about?" I ask.

"That nigga Sam, he cousins with Isaiah and Sean. He said they robbed him," Dave says.

"Well, where Adam at? I want that nigga head on platter," I ask.

"He was the one who robbed Sam with them niggas, he said he saw them last in Crescent Park," Dave says.

"Man, bro, right on, I'm about to call my Unc and let him know," I say.

"It's all good, bro, I know Bobby would've done the same if that was me," Dave says.

*****

Five niggas in the parking lot shooting dice on Southside Richmond.

"Bet five, nigga," Adam says.

"Bet, nigga," Sean says.

"What's yo point, nigga?" Adam says.

"How you gone bet me and don't know my point, bitch nigga?" Sean says. "Because you ain't gone hit no way, pussy. So what's yo point?" Adam says. "Nigga, it's five," Sean say.

"Bet another five on five-nine seven-eleven," Adam says.

"It's good," Sean says.

"Let's go. Niggas wanna give out free money today, and a nigga trying get some new jays," Sean says as he shakes up the dice and rolls a four.

"Damn! Come on, baby, gain one pound," Sean says as he gathers the dice and rolls again and rolls a nine.

"That's what I'm talking about bet it back," Sean says as he hits nine and wins the side bet.

"Yup. It's all good," Adam says as he drops another five. Sean gathers the dice and rolls again and rolls a five.

"Told y'all niggas y'all gone buy my J's today," Sean says as he hits his point and collects everybody money.

"Fuck you, nigga, I got you faded bet ten on yo let go," Adam says.

"It's all good, mo money! Mo money! Daddy need a new fit with them Jays," Sean says as he rolls a seven.

"Aaaaahhhhh! Nigga give me money!" Sean yells.

"Nigga, them dice loaded, let me see them," Adam says.

"Nigga, if they loaded then you must've tried to get over last time we shot dice cause these the same ones we was shooting with before you got the call about Twan," Isaiah says. Which is one of the other five niggas.

"Nigga, what you mean I left those there," Adam says.

"Yeah, I know I grabbed them when y'all left" Isaiah says.

"Did y'all ever find out who did that to Twan?" Sam asks. Which is the fourth person of the five niggas.

"Naw. OG Nitz-O said he gone find out who did it, he said it had to be them niggas from northside," Adam says.

"Man where that nigga Jordan at? I ain't seen that nigga all day. How he taking his brother death?" Carl asks. He is the fifth person. Adam and Sean looks at each other when they hear that.

"Shit I don't know, I ain't talk to that nigga all day. I kept calling his phone and he didn't answer," Adam says.

"Man I hope he all good cause I know I was mad as hell when my older brother died" Carl says. "Didn't yo brother get smacked by the police?" Adam says.

"Yeah, he had a BB gun on him, and they thought it was a real gun. Nigga was only thirteen," Carl says.

"Man I ain't gone lie, I heard the twins' uncle had that boy hit," Sam says.

"Which twins?" Isaiah asks.

"Lil Bobby and Michael," Sam answers.

"Man that nigga ain't do shit he not even with the shit like that," Adam says.

"Who you talking about, nigga?" Sam asks.

"The twins' uncle, that nigga's a fake bitch on the mob nigga," Adam responds.

"Shit I heard he was laying niggas down back in the day and still is now I see," Sam says.

"Nigga, you tryna be funny 'bout my cuddy gettin' hit?" Adam asks.

"Naw, nigga, you know I fucked with Twan, tough don't even be coming at me like that," Sam says.

"Twan wouldn't of even known you if you wasn't hanging around us, so don't act like you knew my cousin," Adam replies.

"Nigga, you always getting mad when you lose some money in the dice game. Be cool before I go get that nigga Lil Bobby to whoop yo ass again. I heard he beat yo ass this morning," Sam says.

"Bitch, what you say?" Adam asks.

"Never mind, bro, it's all good. Let's just shoot some dice," Sam says.

"Naw, nigga, you feeling yoself today, say what you said again, bro, so I can knock the shit out of you," Adam says.

Sam laughs.

"Nigga, you ain't 'bout to bust a grape," Sam says as he turns his head to give Sean a fade.

Adam then pulls out his gun from his waistband and points it at the back of Sam's head.

"Nigga! What's that shit you was talking bitch?" Adam says.

"Nigga, be cool, I was just playing, damn," Sam says with his hands up shaking like he's having a seizure.

"Yeah, nigga, that's what I thought. You just like that nigga Bobby when I had that nigga just like this," Adam says.

"Bro, I was just kidding, damn! You know you my nigga," Sam says.

"Matter fact, run all that in yo pockets, nigga," Adam says.

"Y'all niggas ain't gone do nothing, y'all just gone let this nigga do this?" Sam says. As he looks at his cousin Sean and Isaiah as they stand still and don't do nothing.

"Nigga, don't look at them, they the only reason I don't smoke yo punk ass right now," Adam says.

"Bro, you ain't got to do lil cuddy like that," Isaiah says, trying to step in.

"Nigga, back up. He running all that in his pockets. He talk a big game, but now he shook with this thang in his face," Adam says as he points the gun at Isaiah.

"Nigga, you better get that shit out my face. You tripping cause you caught yo first body," Isaiah says.

"Nigga, wat u mean? I been laying niggas down that nigga Bobby was just another trophy," Adam brags, pointing the gun back at Sam.

"Yeah? Who else you bodied nigga please tell me?" Isaiah asks.

"Nigga, I ain't gonna tell you nothing, what you the feds?" Adam says.

"Nigga, fuck you, you know I ain't no feds I just don't like how niggas be tryna act hard when they got a gun," Isaiah says.

"Well, the nigga shouldn't of been talking shit. He ain't even from this side anyway. If I don't jack this nigga, somebody else from our side gone get him, so why not get this nigga before they do? So run that shit, nigga, I ain't stutter," Adam says pointing the gun in Sam's face.

Sam takes out 1,500 dollars and a half zip of weed and takes off his gold chain and gold rings.

"Y'all acting like we ain't talk about robbing this nigga before, y'all just mad I put in action," Adam says.

"Yeah, nigga, but we should've planned some other day. You hot right now, bro," Sean says.

"So you was gone rob me cuddy?" Sam asks.

"Nigga, I don't even like fucking with you. That be Isaiah wanting you around, and nigga you ain't do shit when yo niggas jumped me at the mall where was you at then, cuddy?" Sean says.

"Nigga, I told you I ain't know that was you they was jumping," Sam says.

"Yeah, okay, nigga. Just give up the shit and get up out of here, and don't come back around here," Sean says.

Chapter 15

I'm Ready

Ring! Ring! Ring!

"Hello?" Dave answers.

"Bro, these niggas just robbed me in the dice game!" Sam yells.

"Nigga, who the fuck is this?" Dave says.

"Nigga, it's me! Sam!" Sam replies.

"Oh. Nigga who robbed you? And where you at?" Dave asks.

"My cousins and that Nigga Adam, they just robbed me in Crescent Park," Sam says.

"Nigga, what the fuck you was doing over there? Yo ass needed to be robbed?" Dave says.

"My cousins hit me asking to shoot with them, and they niggas I shot with them before I thought it was all good to shoot again," Sam says.

"Wait, hold up, who the niggas you said robbed you?" Dave asks.

"My cousins Sean and Isaiah they from the south side," Sam says.

"Naw, the other nigga you said," Dave asks.

"Oh, that nigga Adam. You told me that nigga Bobby beat up," Sam says.

"Bro, that bitch nigga just killed Bobby!" Dave says.

"What Bobby?" Sam asks.

"Nigga, my best friend Bobby. Where that nigga at?" Dave asks.

"Shit! I didn't know he was talking about that Bobby. Them niggas was just at the park last time I seen them when they robbed me," Sam says.

"Nigga, you sure that it was him?" Dave says.

"Yeah, the nigga with dreads, dark skin, tall and lanky with a tattoo on his neck," Sam says.

"Damn, nigga, what you write a biography on that nigga?" Dave says.

"Naw, nigga, I just remembered what he looked like. So what happen to Bobby?" Sam asks.

"Shit, all I can say is that me and Michael saw that bitch nigga kill Bobby cold blooded in the face with three other niggas," Dave says.

"Who was the other niggas?" Sam asks.

"I don't know about the other two niggas, but that nigga Bobby knocked one of them out before he died. His name was Jordan," Dave says.

"Ain't that Twan little brother?" Sam asks.

"Yeah, Michael was beating the shit out that nigga till the police came," Dave says.

"So y'all don't know who the other people was? What they look like?" Sam asks.

"Nigga, I just said I didn't see them, but they was light skinned, both of them was," Dave says.

"Was they tall or short?" Sam asks.

"Lightweight tall, one of them looked dead-on Sean, yo cousin," Dave says.

"Bro, that's why I'm asking because them niggas was just talking about some shit like Bobby being his first body and how they had that nigga begging for his life like a bitch and shit," Sam explains.

"So yo cousins was the niggas that was holding Bobby?" Dave asks.

"Shit, I don't know. They didn't say that they had anything to do with it, but I ain't gone put it past them. That nigga Sean always following Adam like a little bitch, and Isaiah always tryna be like Sean," Sam says.

"Bro, them niggas gone die for what they did to my nigga," Dave says.

"Bro, I know my cousins had something to do with it, and I know you gonna go tell Michael 'bout this, but try to tell them to not hurt my cousins although they fucked up and robbed me. They still family, and that nigga Isaiah ain't really with the shit. He got a scholarship to college, he just probably got mixed up in some shit because of his brother," Sam says, trying to explain.

"Nigga, my nigga Bobby wasn't going to college or nothing like that, but he was going somewhere. Now he ain't even here to see another day, so fuck that nigga Adam and yo bitch-ass cousins, bro! They made they own deathbeds," Dave says.

"Yeah. You right, bro. So wassup? You gone come pick me up, bro?" Sam says.

"Nigga, is that why you called this whole time? And do you got gas money?" Dave says.

"Yeah, and naw, they just hit me. How I'ma have some gas money?" Sam says.

"All right, bro. Give me ten minutes, and I'll come swoop you," Dave says.

"Fasho, bro, can you bring some chips and soda for me?" Sam asks.

"Sure, you want some steak and lobster too?" Dave asks.

"Naw. I'll take a burrito," Sam says.

Phone clicks.

"Hello? Dave! Hello?" Sam says.

Ring! Ring! Ring!

"If you ain't calling to tell me you found that nigga don't speak," Unc Stino says.

"Unc, it's me Michael," I say.

"Oh, wassup, nephew? You good?" Unc Stino says.

"Naw, Mom's tried to throw a bottle at me and tryna tell me it's all my fault that Bobby is dead," I say.

"Don't even pay her no mind, lil nigga, she just going through it right now, losing your brother and shit," Unc Stino says.

"Yeah, she was telling me not to trust you and how you not our real uncle and other stuff," I say.

"She said all that with a glass in her hand I bet," Unc Stino says.

"Man, you know she did her drunk ass even forgot to go pick up Donny from school," I say.

"Wait, so Donny still at school?" Unc Stino asks.

"Naw, I just picked him up. I had to tell him 'bout Bobby," I say.

"How is he taking it?" Unc Stino asks.

"He over here crying now. At first he didn't believe me," I explain.

"Well, y'all don't worry yo Unc gon find the nigga that did this to Bobby and make him pay," Unc Stino says.

"Speaking of him, that's why I was calling you I know where them niggas at," I say.

"What niggas?" Unc Stino says.

"The niggas that killed my brother, all three of them," I say.

"What you mean all three, and where they at?" Unc Stino asks.

"Unc! No offense, but I want these niggas dead by my hands just like they took my brother," I say.

"Lil nigga, you ain't ready for this life, so just let me handle this. Just tell where they at," Unc Stino says.

"Naw Unc, I am ready, and I'm tired of y'all thinking I'm not. You was willing to let Bobby kill someone, so why can't I?" I say.

"Because Bobby hood mentality, you brain smart, and these streets ain't for you to be in," Unc Stino explains.

"Nigga, you the one who brought us up in this life, and these streets may not be meant for me but these streets took my brother and my father, and none of them has had justice. And it's 'bout time I changed that," I say.

"They did catch the nigga who killed your dad, and he's rotting in prison for the rest of his life for it," Unc Stino says.

"Well, that ain't enough for me. After I kill them niggas that got Bobby, I'ma make sure the nigga that killed my dad suffer too," I say.

"So you really think you ready for this life, Mike?" Unc Stino asks.

"Yes. I am. Now can you come pick us up so we can go get these niggas?" I ask.

"Nigga, what you mean us? Lil D ain't coming with us, he going home," Unc Stino says.

"Aww, man, come on, Unc, I want that nigga dead too," Donny says.

"Hell naw, it's bad enough I'm taking Michael. I'll be damn if I take you too," Unc Stino says.

"Man, come on. You act like I ain't seen a dead body before," Lil D says.

"Man, yo dad would've beat my ass knowing I'm doing this." Stino sighs.

"Too bad that nigga dead. So when you coming?" Lil D says. I smack Lil D upside his head.

"Nigga, shut up! Don't be talking bad 'bout Daddy like that," I say.

"Ooooooohh, nigga, don't be hitting me," Lil D says.

"Man, y'all niggas still acting like kids, y'all ain't ready to take no life," Unc Stino says.

"Fuck all that. If you ain't gone come get us, then I'll find my own way to go kill these niggas," I say.

"Hold up, speedy, go kill 'em. Where y'all at?" Unc Stino ask.

"Walking down cutting 'bout to go through the forties," I say.

"Ait'e, give me ten min, I'll be on my way," Unc Stino says.

"If you're not here by then, you just gone be picking up Lil Donny because I'ma be on a mission already," I say, serious as fuck.

"Nigga, how you gone kill him? With what?" Unc Stino asks.

"I got mine, don't worry 'bout me," I say.

"Nigga, who gave you a gun?" Unc Stino asks.

"My daddy did. He told me where it was and told me if he ever died to be the man of the house and get revenge for his death, and that's exactly what I'm gone do," I say.

"Nigga, what I tell you 'bout guns, that's why your dad is dead now. He was always quick to pull the trigger," Unc Stino says.

"Well, thanks for letting me know I'm my daddy's son, and you got six more minutes," I say, looking at my cellphone on a countdown.

"Little nigga, I don't know who you think you fucking talking to, but I ain't one of these lil niggas out here on these streets," Unc Stino says.

"Well, nigga, you acting like you don't want this nigga who killed Bobby dead right now just like you let the nigga who killed my dad still breathe," I say, letting him know what's really on my mind.

"Little nigga, I'm warning you, I'm not the one to be fucked with. You should know that, so choose yo next words carefully," Unc Stino suggests.

"Naw, you know what maybe my mom's is right. Maybe we do look up to you just a bit too much. Bobby is really dead because of you. If you never would've told Bobby you killed Twan, he would still be alive," I say.

"So now it's my fault Bobby's dead, huh? Y'all know what? I've been taking care of y'all niggas since y'all daddy died, making sure y'all always straight and got food and money in y'all pockets, and this the thanks I get," Unc Stino says.

"You act like we asked you to do anything. Ain't nobody ask you for shit, then and I'm not now," I say.

"Nigga, you asking me for a ride now," Unc Stino says.

"Like I said, you had ten minutes to get here, so now you can just pick up Donny, and you ain't got to worry 'bout me," I say.

"Naw, nigga, I ain't got to worry 'bout none of y'all niggas" Unc Stino says, firm.

"In that case leave us the fuck alone, you bitch nigga, I'm gone take care of us from now on. We don't need shit from you anymore," I say as I hang up the phone.

"Hello! Hello? Michael, I know this nigga didn't just hang up on me," Stino says.

CHAPTER 16

MYSTERY MAN

Ring! Ring! Ring!

"Hello?" a voice on the phone says.

"Where the fuck you at?" Stino says.

"Well, hello to you too, Stino," the voice on the phone says.

"Nigga, I ain't got time for your games. Did you find that nigga Adam yet?" Stino asks.

"If I did, I think I would've been the one calling you," the voice on the phone says.

"Well, this nigga Michael found out where Adam is," Stino says.

"That's good. How he find him, and why the fuck you calling me if you already knew where he was?" the voice on the phone says.

"Nigga, he didn't tell me where Adam was, he said he wanted to handle it on his own. That nigga started spazzin' out talking 'bout I'm the reason Lil Bobby dead," Stino says.

"Ummmm, nigga, and you don't think you are the reason he is?" the voice on the phone says.

"Hell naw, I didn't think that nigga would be yapping his mouth like he was, so how's that my fault he couldn't back it up?" Stino says.

"Bro, let's be real. You cursed them niggas just like we was when was growing up in the hood introducing them to drug game at young age. Living that life you either end up dead, jail, or still hustling like yo black ass," the voice on the phone says.

"Nigga, if it wasn't for me, them niggas would be in the systems. You know damn well Eve wasn't gone take care of them you remember that time she was drinking and passed out at home and left that nigga Donny in the tub when he was one. I'm the one that stayed by that nigga side at the hospital for two weeks," Stino says.

"Well, if David was here, he'll be very proud of you," the voice on the phone says as he laughs.

"Nigga, fuck you, naw but for real, we need to find this nigga Adam before this nigga Michael do," Stino says.

"Why don't you just call that nigga and ask him where he at so you can leave me alone?" the voice on the phone says.

"Nigga, his phone going straight to voicemail, that's why I'm calling you so you can track it," Stino says.

"Hold on," the voice on the phone says.

"He must've broke it. I can't locate his location nowhere, smart kid so how is he supposedly posed to kill Adam? With his hands?" the voice on the phone asks.

"He said David told him where a gun was before he died and to avenge his death or some shit like that," Stino says.

"Nigga, what gun?" the voice on the phone says.

"Nigga, I don't know, some gun I got too mad to ask 'bout it."

"You should've heard the way that nigga was talking, I swear that nigga remind me so much of David, it's crazy," Stino says.

"Nigga, stop crying like a bitch. You need to find out what type of gun it is because what if it's the hood gun from back in the day?" the voice on the phone says.

"Nigga, that gun been gone, you said you been got rid of it," Stino says.

"No, nigga, I never saw it after the last time we used it on the migos in central." Maybe that nigga David took it," the voice on the phone says.

"Nigga, so what if it is the same gun? That nigga hands on it now," Stino says.

"Nigga, if it is the same gun, that shit can put us in jail for years. Just because his hands on it, don't mean our old fingerprints ain't still on there," the voice on the phone says.

"Now who sound like a bitch? You worried 'bout your old life coming back up again, nigga, don't forget that old life is the reason you have the life you have now," Stino says.

"You ain't gotta tell me how the fuck I got somewhere. I know how I got here, but I'll be damn if I let my past come fuck me over now," the voice on the phone says.

"Yeah, I hear you. I'll be damn if I let this nigga David snitch on us from the dead," Stino says.

"All right, let me make a few phone calls to see what I can find out, and I'll call you back," the voice says.

*****

Ring! Ring!
"Hello?" Virgil says.

"Hello? Mr. Virgil," the connect says.

"Man, what I tell you 'bout saying my name like that? It sounds creepy coming out of your mouth," Virgil says.

"Why, Mr. Virgil?" the connect says.

"Because you sound like a person that wants my soul," Virgil says.

"Nigga, you somkin that shit, ain't you?"

"Indeed," Virgil says while laughing.

"As long as you got my money, you can do whatever you want," the connect says.

"Man, chill. You sound so tense, and of course, I got your money. Have I ever not had it?" Virgil says as he starts coughing.

"Yeah, you forgot to pay two weeks ago, and I had to send my people to see if you were okay, you don't remember that?" the connect says.

"Why you always gotta bring up old shit, I told you my phone broke and lost yo number," Virgil says.

"Whatever, nigga! Where's my money?" the connect says.

"I got it right here, man, but I'ma need some more of them cookies and some more zans and another pack," Virgil says.

"Same deal as last time, seven thousand. Half now and the rest on delivery," the connect says.

"All good, so can you get more Glocks and Mac-10s this time? Cause that last pack was bunk with all them 9 mm," Virgil says.

"See, that's what's wrong with y'all generation messing with all them jammers, y'all don't know nothing 'bout guns," the connect says.

"Yeah, yeah, whatever, old head. So how much I owe you?" Virgil says.

"That's gone be thousand unless you want some of this new gelato, I got it's way better than the cookies," the connect says.

"Man, stop lying, ain't nothing better than them cookies," Virgil says.

"Wanna bet? That shit is some dope, it will knock yo ass out with one blunt," the connect says.

"Man, let me try it!" Virgil says.

"It's gone be extra because I paid top dollar for that," the connect says.

"How much extra?" Virgil asks.

"Shit, give me 7,500, and I'll make sure they hook you up down there," the connect says.

"Man, that shit better be good too. I need some real good to smoke to take my mind off not going back home and beat this nigga ass again," Virgil says.

"What's wrong? Found a nigga in bed with yo bitch?" the connect asks sarcastically.

"Man, hell naw. What would make you say some dumb shit like that?" Virgil asks.

"Trust me, she ain't worth it," the connect says.

"Nigga, I'm talking 'bout my little brother," Virgil says.

"What? He been in yo shit again?" the connect says.

"Yeah, he is, and this little nigga let some niggas rob him for some weed he took from me. Some money too," Virgil explains.

"You know how this game goes, he was bound to get jumped one of these days," the connect says.

"Yeah, it's just crazy because two of the little niggas our cousins, that's why he was over there," Virgil says.

"Damn so his cousins robbed him? That's some fucked-up shit," the connect asks.

"Naw, he said some nigga whipped out on him in the dice game and stripped him in front of everybody. One of our cousins was helping, and the other was just looking," Virgil says.

"Wait! So why you mad at that little nigga for shooting dice with his family? The nigga that robbed him probably got hit in the game, wanted his money back and more," the connect sys.

"Because that nigga should've known better to go to the Crescents," Virgil says.

"Man, all that little nigga gotta do is catch them slipping one at a time and give them his hands," the connect says.

"Oh, he gone fasho do that. I told him its either he beat they ass, or I'm beating his," Virgil says.

"Do he know the person who whipped out on him is?" the connect says.

"Yeah, he said some nigga that was related to Twan, I think his name like Adam or something like that," Virgil says.

"Do you mean Twan Lil cousin Adam from the manor?" the connect says.

"Yeah, I think that's him. Why you know him?" Virgil says.

"Yeah, I heard of him. Word around town that he the one who killed little Bobby and Stino been looking for him all day," the connect says.

"Wait hold up, not little Bobby from north?" Virgil asks.

"Yup, he got smacked this morning," the connect says.

"Damn, that's crazy. That little nigga was just over my house two days ago playing madden with my little brother," Virgil says.

"Yeah, you know this nigga Stino gonna go on a rampage now over that little nigga," the connect says.

"Man, I'm already knowing shit. I guess my brother ain't gone have no chance to get that nigga before Stino do," Virgil says.

"Yeah, because the way that nigga Stino sounded on the phone, he is as good as dead," the connect says.

"Damn. That's crazy for little Brodie to be gone, he was a funny little nigga, always tryna play with my favorite gun," Virgil says.

"Yeah, well, you know how it goes. You live by the gun, you die by the gun," the connect says.

"Damn OG, you ain't got no heart for the youth," Virgil says.

"Naw, just not for the ones that don't stick to the hood code, its rules to this game and y'all generation don't respect it," the connect says.

"Well shit, when can I come get that?" Virgil says.

"Give me an hour. I'll have it ready for you to pick up at the same spot you picked it up last time," the connect says.

"A'ite. Bet so I heard that nigga Twan was hit for snitching on Stino," Virgil says.

"Shit, I heard that nigga Twan was visiting somebody in jail that Stino didn't fuck with, and Twan acted like he didn't care, so Stino dealt with him," the connect says.

"Damn, that's crazy I fucked with Twan. I used to play baseball with him for Richmond Little League. I heard he had a baby on the way too," Virgil says.

"Another victim to the hood curse," the connect says.

"What's that you talking 'bout now, old man?" Virgil asks.

"The hood curse is a curse that is placed on every child who is born in the hood environment," the connect says.

"So what they cursed with?" Virgil asks.

"Listen, youngster, they are cursed on living from the bottom of the food chain of this world. You ever wonder why nobody can make it past eighteen?" the connect explains.

"Well, I got a couple more months before I'm up to yo status, so I ain't trippin," Virgil says.

"And how you figure that, youngster?" The connect asks.

"I'ma be a OG," Virgil says.

"Ahahahahahhha!" the connect laughs on the phone.

"What's so funny?" Virgil asks.

"Nothing, youngster. You just brought up some past memories," the connect says.

"Whatever, man, I'ma be a OG and all these niggas gone respect me," Virgil says.

"Okay, youngster. Just make sure none of the shit you get into come back to me, 'cause if it does, I'm coming for you," the connect says.

"It's all good, man, why you always gotta be so serious all the time?" Virgil says.

"Because, I'm serious 'bout my money, and I refused to let a pothead little nigga ruin my shit," the connect says.

"A'ite, brah. Just hit me when my pack ready, I'll hit you in two weeks to reup," Virgil explains.

"Okay," Mr. Virgil the connect says.

"Mannn, fuck you," Virgil says.

Phone clicks.

"Hello? Hello? I know this nigga ain't hang up," Virgil says.

Chapter 17

Let's Ride

Ring! Ring! Ring! Ring!

"Hello?" Dave says.

"Aye, Dave Bro. It's Michael. Where you at?" I say.

"Damn, nigga, y'all did it that quick? Unc wasn't doin' no playing," Dave says.

"Man, fuck that nigga. He act like he the only one that wanna kill that nigga Adam. Telling me I'm not ready for that life, he don't know shit," I say.

"Bro, what the fuck happen, y'all didn't go kill him?" Dave says.

"Naw, I was trying to go with my Unc to go kill him, but he was acting like a bitch, so I didn't tell him where Adam was," I say.

"So what you gonna do now?" Dave asks.

"That's why I called you, bro, you the only person that I know I can trust because Bobby trusted you, and I know you would ride for Bobby, so I'm asking you to ride with me to go get these niggas," I tell Dave.

"When you tryna do it?" Dave asks hesitantly.

"Right now," I say.

"How many hammas you got?" Dave asks.

"I only got one on me, but all I needed for you to do is drive, bro, I'ma do the shooting," I say.

"Bro, come to my house! We hot talking like this on the phone. I'ma call my boy Sam, I know his big brothers got some extra hammas," Dave says.

"All right, bro, we on our way to you now," I say.

"Nigga, who is we?" Dave asks.

"Me and Donny," I say.

"Nigga, you got Lil D with you? How we supposed to go ride with yo lil brother?" Dave says.

"Lil D deserves to be there just as much as anybody else. He need to see the nigga that took our brother suffer for what he did," I say.

"Bro, I ain't tryna go to jail over your brother snitching on us," Dave says.

"Bro, don't worry, he not gone say nothing," I say.

"A'ite, how long before y'all get here?" Dave asks.

"The taxi five minutes away," I say.

"Nigga, how we riding on these niggas?" Dave asks.

"I know where we can get a stolo," I tell him.

"A'ite, Bet. See y'all in a minute," Dave says.

The taxi car drops me and Donny off in the hill. We both get out the cab quick and start knocking on the door.

"What's the password?" Dave asks sarcastically.

"Nigga, ain't no password," I respond.

"You sure? I thought we had a password," Dave says, still behind the closed door. "Nigga, stop playing, it's cold as fuck out here," I tell him.

"A'ite! A'ite! Wasup, niggas?" Dave says as he opens the door.

"Nigga, you play too much," I say.

"What, you don't check and see who at your door before you let them in?" Dave asks.

"Of course, we do, but we don't ask for a password to come in," I say.

"Well, sorry my mama raised me a lil different," Dave explains.

"Whatever, nigga! Where yo potna at?" I say.

"Oh, that nigga Sam? He said he was gon grab some hammas from his brother stash," Dave says.

"Damn, his brother ain't gon notice?" I ask.

"Naw, his brother don't even be noticing when we be taking his weed. And besides, it ain't like we stealing them, we just gone use them and put them back so he would never know," Dave explains.

"Who his brother?" I ask.

"Virgil," Dave answers.

"Nigga, you talking 'bout Virgil from the hill?" I say.

"Yup, that's him." Dave nods.

"That's what's up. So I'm guessing Sam a shooter like his brother, huh?" I ask but really was assuming.

"I don't know if he shot anybody or nothing like that, but I know when I called him, he was down to ride on them niggas for robbing him earlier today," Dave answers honestly.

"I thought you said he was they cousin?" I ask, trying to be clear.

"He said that family shit went out the door when they robbed him, and I guess he told his brother because he was hot 'bout that shit too," Dave says.

"Damn, well, it's all good, he ain't gone snitch on us if he go down, is he?" I ask seriously.

"That's not who I'm worried about snitching on us," Dave says.

"Who you think gone snitch on us?" I ask.

Dave looks at Lil D. "If we do this shit, how we know yo Brother ain't gon get scared and tell on us after? I don't think he should come. He can just stay here, and we can pick him up on the way back," Dave suggests.

"Naw, man, I'm going. I want to see that nigga die for what he did to Bobby," Lil D says.

"You too young to be seeing shit like this, lil bro," Dave says.

"First off I'm not yo brother, and second off, I done seen plenty dead bodies before. Shit, I seen Twan body this morning, so ain't no different seeing the man who killed my real brother dying in front of me. At least it would give Bobby some justice," Lil D says.

"All right, lil nigga, you think you ready for this life. But if I go to jail over yo ass, I'ma get you," Dave says.

"Nigga, you ain't gone do shit to my brother," I say.

"Nigga, I'm just playing, damn. Take a joke," Dave says.

"Why you always making a joke out of something? This shit so serious right now," I say.

The doorbell rings. "Who is it?" Dave asks.

"It's me, nigga," Sam says.

"Me nigga who?" Dave asks.

"Man nigga, stop playing. It's colder than polar bear toenail out here," Sam says.

"What's the password?" Dave continues to play.

"Pineapples," Sam says. And the door opens quickly.

"Sam. My Nigga," Dave says.

"Yeah. Yeah. Yeah, nigga, move it's cold," Sam says as he rushes into the door with a black duffel bag.

"Damn no hand clap, hug, or nothing. Just rude," Dave says.

"Nigga, fuck you. I just seen yo ass a couple hours ago. What's up with y'all niggas though?" Sam says as he acknowledges me and Lil D.

"What's good with you, bro?" I say. Lil D just nods his head toward him.

"I'm sorry to hear what happen to Bobby, that Nigga was hella koo and hella funny," Sam says, trying to lighten the mood.

"Right on, bro, and sorry to hear yo cousins got on you like they did," I say, returning the concern.

"Yeah, them niggas faulty for doing that, and my brother got on me about letting them niggas do that, so now I got to put some respect on my name and show these niggas I'm not the one to be messed with," Sam says.

"Bro, as long as I get to kill that nigga Adam, it's all good," I say.

"It's all good, bro, I ain't trippin. Just make sure you don't miss," Sam says.

"Nigga, please. I got aim," I say.

"Nigga, what you shooting?" Sam asks"

I pull out my 9 mm from my waistband "I got this big bulky thang right here. Pops gave me this before he died," I say as I'm showing it off.

"Okay, bro, I see. You better hope that thang don't jam on you," Dave says.

"Nigga, my dad used this shit all through Richmond. He called it the hood gun, so I know this thang ain't gone jam on me," I say, confident.

"Nigga, do you know how long ago that was? That shit been sitting and got rusted. Man Sam, did you bring my shit?" Dave asks.

"You mean my bro favorite gun? You better make sure ain't no scratch on it this time, cause I had to take the fall for you last time we took it on them central niggas and yo dumb ass dropped it," Sam says.

"Nigga, shut up. You know that was on accident when we was running after them niggas," Dave says.

"Here, nigga," Sam says as he handed Dave a .45 Glock with a woodgrain grip.

"Ohhh baby! How I miss holding you," Dave says.

"Nigga, you stupid," Sam says as he reaches into the bag and pulls out a Glock 40.

"Damn, nigga, you sure yo bro ain't go know we got these?" I say.

"Hell naw, that nigga went to go meet with his connect. As long as we get them back before he get back, we should be good, bro. I got an extra Glock if you ain't tryna use that old thang," Sam says.

"Yeah, man, leave the muffet here and pick up one of these real thangs, so you don't miss that nigga when you kill him," Dave says.

"Man, y'all both got me fucked up. I'm gone make sure I'm the last person he sees on this earth," I say.

"Okay, nigga, but if you take one of these Glocks he got, you got a better chance with it not jamming on you," Dave says.

"All right, fuck it," I says as I put the 9 mm back into my waistline.

"Nigga, just leave it here, and come get it when we done," Dave says.

"Man, you ain't gonna steal my shit," I say.

"Nigga, please, I don't want that death trap. I'm just fine with this baby right here. How you doing, baby? Did you miss me?" Dave says as he talks to the gun he was holding as if it were a baby.

"Nigga, how we gonna go get on these niggas?" Sam asks.

"It's all good. I know where one of my Uncle Stino cars is," I say.

"Shit, we gon have to get the plates off it, so it ain't traced back to him," Sam says.

"They already off. It's one of his cars he use to ride on niggas," I say.

"Nigga, how you know?" Dave asks.

"'Cause, nigga, I listen and I know most of that niggas operation," I say.

"Oh, okay, Mr. Sherlock Holmes," Dave says.

"Fuck you, nigga, I'ma take this one," I say as I grab a gun out the bag.

"Look at this nigga tryna blow a nigga head back with a Desert Eagle. You sure ready for that? It ain't an automatic, and it pack a whole lot of power," Sam says.

"Yeah, this the one right here," I say as I hold the gun in my hand, admiring the chrome shininess.

"Okay, well, let's go do this shit then," Dave says.

"Where my shit at?" Lil D says.

"You just gon sit in the car, Donny, you don't need no gun," I say.

"Wait, hold up. Lil bro going too?" Sam asks.

"Yeah, I told him he should leave him here and not have him go," Dave says.

"Man, I ain't tryna hear all that he going," I say.

"Shit, I ain't got no problem with it. I damn near caught my first body at seven fucking round with my brother. He broke me in the game early. If lil bro riding, he gone need a strap just in case, though, you never know," Sam says.

"What the fuck is wrong with y'all? Am I the only one that think that he don't need to be going?" Dave asks.

"Yup," Sam says. "Here, lil bro, take this .22. It ain't got the much power, but if you got aim it's gone get the job done," Sam continues to say as he hands Lil D the gun.

"Do you even know how to use that, lil nigga?" Dave ask.

Lil Donny cocks back the gun and loads it and points it at Dave. "You tryna find out?" Lil D finally says.

"Nigga, get that shit out my face before I beat yo ass," Dave says as he smacks the gun out of Lil D's hand.

"Man! Can y'all stop playing? It's time to go get these niggas," I say.

"Well, shit, let's ride. I'm ready," Sam says.

Chapter 18

What's the 911?

Ring! Ring! Ring!

"Hello?" Stino says.

"Hello, Mr. Stino," the connect says.

"I hate when you say my name like that," Stino says.

"What's that, Mr. Stino?" the connect says.

"Bye, nigga, I ain't got time for this shit," Stino says.

"Fine then. You don't want to know where Adam is?" the connect says.

"My nigga! You finally came through. Where he at?" Stino says.

"Nuh-uh, naw, Nigga. What's in it for me?" the connect asks.

"What you want, nigga, money?" Stino asks.

"I didn't, but I'll gladly accept that too. But I don't know right now. I guess you'll just owe me one for now," the connect says.

"You know I don't like owing nobody shit," Stino says.

"Well, I guess you can hang up the phone then, as you were about to do," the connect says.

"Man, fine, I'll owe you a favor. Now tell me where he is," Stino says.

"Well, you remember that little nigga Virgil? The one we had to shake up for some money a couple weeks ago?" the connect asks.

"Yeah, what about him?" Stino asks.

"Well, his brother got jumped at a dice game in the Crescents by his cousins," the connect says.

"Damn that's fucked up, but what the fuck that got to do with anything?" Stino asks.

"Well, Virgil said the Nigga who was with the cousins and actually robbed the brother was Adam," the connect says.

"You sure it's the same Adam?" Stino asks.

"Yeah, he said it was Twan little cousin," the connect answers.

"How long ago was this?" Stino says.

"Shit, I don't know. I'm guessing a few hours ago," the connect says.

"Damn, maybe that's how that nigga Michael found out where he was," Stino says.

"Well, what you gone do?" the connect asks.

"I'ma call that nigga Sergio. That nigga be out there in the Crescents, so I'ma see if he seen that nigga out there," Stino says.

"A'ite, good luck," the connect says.

"Nigga, you riding when I go get this nigga?" Stino says.

"You funny as hell. Bye, nigga," the connect says.

"Man whatever. You a behind-the-desk-type nigga now," Stino says.

"Naw. I was just always smarter than you," the connect says.

"So you say, nigga, I bet you forgot how to shoot anyway," Stino says.

"Wanna find out? Keep running your mouth, I'll put another BB gun to your cheek and send you the hospital again," the connect says.

"Fuck you, nigga," Stino says.

The connect starts laughing, but the phone clicks.

Ring! Ring! Ring!

"Hola!" Sergio answers, speaking Spanish.

"Serg! My nigga, what's good with you?" Stino asks.

"Who is this?" Sergio asks.

"It's me, man, Stino," Stino answers.

"Stino my man! What's going on homez? Long time no talk, man. What's new with you?" Sergio asks.

"Aww, man, I can't call it, tryna keep this money coming in. You know how it is out here in the hood, somebody gotta keep it coming," Stino says.

Sergio begins to laugh. "Still the same Stino the Kilo, I see."

"You know I ain't gone never change," Stino says.

"Yeah, I hear you, man. That money makes everyone feel like kings, but you know we only have one king," Sergio says.

"Damn, Serge the Purge, looks like I ain't the only one that ain't changed. You still preaching over there on cutting," Stino asks.

"You know the Lord always been speaking through me, using me as a weapon on these streets of Richmond to let our people know who is the Almighty," Sergio says.

Stino laughs hella loud.

Sergio starts to laugh too.

"Naw, wassup, nigga?" Sergio asks.

"Shit, man, I been looking for this little nigga named Adam," Stino says.

"Does this have something to do with the death of David little boy?" Sergio asks, concerned.

"Yeah, I found out that he was the nigga that killed him, and he was last seen in the Crescents," Stino informed Sergio.

"Well I'll ask around, and I'm sorry 'bout little Bobby. I was sad to hear that he died from my daughter. She was pretty upset 'bout his death as well," Sergio says.

"Okay, please do, and thank you. How's little Keisha by the way?" Stino asks.

"Man, she just better be glad I'm a preacher because I would've been killed her. I wish she would've never grown up," Sergio says, honestly.

"Man tell me 'bout it. Raising kids is a headache, but let me know something if you find out anything," Stino says.

"Okay, I'm at the church house right now handling some business. I'll make a few calls and get back to you if I hear something," Sergio says.

"Right on, man. And let me ask you something. How much of that God money you be making on Sundays?" Stino asks.

"Brother, I can't say all that over the phone, but I can say I got about four hundred people coming in, and 'bout three hundred out of the four hundred give me their tithes, which is 10 percent of all of their income earnings. So that's about sixty and up, and mind you I have three services on Sunday," Sergio says.

"Damn, if this hood shit don't work out, I know what my next career path is," Stino says.

"May God bless you and your path, my brother," Sergio says.

"Ahahahha, nope never mind you can keep that fake shit," Stino says.

"Ahahahahahah, I'ma holla at you, brother," Sergio says.

"Right on, man," Stino says before hanging up.

Chapter 19

Caught Up!

"Man, pass that shit," Adam says.

"Damn, nigga. I just got it," Sean says as he puffs on a blunt full of cookies.

"Man, you ain't even put in on this," Adam says.

"Nigga like you spent any money on this shit," Sean says.

"Nigga, I'm the one who robbed the nigga. Y'all niggas froze up. If it wasn't for me, y'all Niggas would've been smoking that bunk-ass shake y'all been smoking on for weeks," Adam says.

"Nigga, we bought that shit from you, so what you talking 'bout?" Isaiah says.

Adam starts laughing out loud. "I know, huh?" he says as he continues laughing.

"That shit isn't funny, nigga, you been hot all day. First you kill Bobby and then you rob our cousin," Isaiah says.

"Nigga, tell the whole world already!" Adam says as he take a drink of a 750 ml bottle of Henny.

"Nigga, we said we was gone jump that nigga, not kill him, OG ain't gone be koo with this," Isaiah says.

"Man, I don't care what OG Nitz-O say, ain't nobody ever seen that nigga in person anyway, so he ain't gone do shit," Adam says.

"Yeah, okay, nigga, you acting all hard just because you got that gun on you," Isaiah says.

"Yeah, nigga, I'm the one with the hamma, what you gone do?" Adam asks.

"Nigga, you wouldn't even have that hamma if Jordan didn't give it to you," Isaiah says.

"So what, they took my cousin from us, and I took one of theirs. OG should be proud of me knockin' that nigga down, he was competition," Adam says.

"Nigga to who? You don't even sell!" Isaiah says.

"Nigga, to the south side Richmond! Fuck them niggas across the tracks. The less of them niggas it is, it's more money for us!" Adam says.

"But that nigga Bobby was only sixteen," Isaiah says.

"So what, nigga? And now he up there with his daddy. If anything, the nigga should be thanking me because it was bound to happen anyway," Adam says as he takes another sip.

"Man, do you here yo boy?" Isaiah says to his brother Sean.

"In a way he do makes sense," Sean says.

"Nigga what? You stay riding that nigga dick. He just made yo dumbass rob your own cousin who we've known since we was babies," Isaiah says angrily."

"Nigga, you ain't do shit neither, so what you talking 'bout?" Sean asks.

"Nigga, what the fuck you talking 'bout? I tried to stop the nigga, but then the nigga want to get gun happy and point that shit my way, which I'd advise you never to do again," Isaiah says.

"Nigga, you sounding like a bitch. Here, tap this Henny and put some hair on your chest," Adam says.

"Fuck y'all niggas. I don't want none of that shit," Isaiah says as he starts walking away.

"Nigga, where you going?" Adam asks.

"Nigga, to take a piss. Is that okay with you, or you gone shoot me over that too?" Isaiah says as he puts his hands in the air.

"Maybe," Adam says as his phone rings.

"Why you ain't been answering my calls, nigga?" Keisha says.

"Baby, my phone been dead after I talked to you earlier. What's up with you, Ma?" Adam says.

"Nigga don't 'Ma' me. Did you kill Bobby?" Keisha says.

"Baby, why would you say some shit like that?" Adam says.

"Because you was asking me all them questions 'bout him," Keisha says.

"Hell naw, I ain't kill him. I didn't even know he was dead till just now," Adam says.

"Yeah. My girl Mary told me he was shot at school by four niggas. One of them got caught," Keisha explains.

"Damn, that's crazy!" Adam says.

"Yeah, I heard they uncle looking for them niggas now," Keisha says.

Beep. Beep. Beep.

"Hold on, babe, it's my dad," Keisha says right before clicking over to answer the other line.

"Hola, Papi," Keisha says.

"Hey, mija. How's my angel?" Sergio says.

"I'm okay, at home bored. When are you coming home, Papi?" Keisha asks.

"I'm at church still, my dear, it's going to be another late one. Where is your mother?" Sergio says.

"She said she was going out with some friends," Keisha responds.

"Did she say with who?" Sergio says.

"I think she said Jessica, one of the mothers from church," Keisha says.

"Are you sure, dear?" Sergio asks.

"I'm pretty sure, Daddy, why?" Keisha says.

"No reason, dear, but I called you to ask you a question," Sergio says.

"What's up, Dad?" Keisha asks.

"Do you know a guy named Adam from the manor?" Sergio asks. Keisha goes silent because she thinks he knows 'bout her and Adam going out.

"Noo, no, Papi. Why do you ask?" Keisha asks.

"You remember Bobby? The young dude that got killed this morning?" Sergio asks.

"Yeah, I remember," Keisha responds.

"Well, word around town is that he had something to do with it," Sergio explains.

"Are you serious, Daddy?" Keisha asks.

"Yeah, baby girl, and I remember hearing you mention his name once on the phone," Sergio says.

"What? Why are you listening to my phone conversations, Dad?" Keisha asks.

"Keisha, you're my daughter, and until you can get your own money to pay for your own phone bills, I will listen to whatever and whoever I want in my house," Sergio says.

"But Daddy, that's not right. I have privacy," Keisha says.

"Well, your privacy is my privacy. How 'bout that?" Sergio says.

"Ugghhhh! I hate you," Keisha says.

"Whatever, little girl, you will get over it. So do you know him or not?" Sergio asks.

"No, Papi, I don't," Keisha says.

"Are you sure? Don't be lying to me because I will find out," Sergio says.

"I mean, I know him, but I don't know him all like that," Keisha says.

"Well, do you know where he is right now?" Sergio asks.

"No, I don't," Keisha answers.

"Okay, baby girl. I'm trusting you don't let me find out you did know where he was, or that's your ass," Sergio says.

"Bye, Dad," Keisha says.

"I love you, baby girl," Sergio says.

Keisha clicks back over to Adam.

"You a motherfucking lie!" Keisha says.

"Babe, what the fuck you talking 'bout now?" Adam asks.

"You did kill Bobby," Keisha says.

"Why do you keep saying that?" Adam says.

"Nigga, because my daddy just called me asking did I know you. At first, I thought he knew 'bout me and you, but then he told me that you had something to do with Bobby being killed," Keisha says.

"Baby, he lying. I ain't touch that nigga, somebody must be spreading lies about me," Adam says.

"Yeah, whatever, nigga. Well, you should know everyone looking for you," Keisha says.

"I don't know why because I ain't did shit all day," Adam continues to lie.

"So where you at? I thought you was coming over today," Keisha says.

"Shit, I'm with my boys right now. Is your daddy working late again?" Adam says.

"Yes he is, and my mom went out again," Keisha says.

"All right, babe, I'ma call you when I'm on my way. Have that pussy ready for Daddy," Adam says.

"Tell Keisha wassup," Isaiah says as he starts walking back from taking a piss.

"Nigga, why the fuck would I tell my woman hi for yo ass?" Adam says.

"Nigga, you act like I wasn't fucking with her before you," Isaiah says.

"Nigga, so y'all was in the past. Nigga, now she my woman. You want problems?" Adam asks as he lifts his shirt to show the gun on his waistband.

"Nigga, I told you try that shit again with that weak-ass gun. Can it even be yours first?" Isaiah says as he starts to get mad.

"Nigga, what I been on this gun-play shit what you talking 'bout?" Adam says.

"Nigga, if Twan didn't get killed today, you wouldn't even have that gun, and that nigga Bobby would still be alive. You ain't nothing but a little bitch, and bro I don't even know why you hang around this nigga. He ain't even with the shit, he just born in it," Isaiah says.

"Nigga, you sounding real hard right now. You better shut up before I shut you up," Adam says as he starts pulling out the gun.

"Nigga, you pull that gun out on me again, you best be ready to use it" Isaiah says as walks up closer to Adam.

"Damn, y'all niggas need to chill out here. Isaiah, hit the blunt," Sean says.

"Yeah, hit the blunt, little nigga, and listen to your brother," Adam says.

"Nigga, fuck you, that's why everybody fucking on your bitch. Why you thinking you the only one? Even Sean hit that shit," Isaiah says.

"Bro," Sean says.

"Nigga, you fucked Keisha too?" Adam says to Sean.

"It was only one time, bro, we was all drunk at this party and shit got wild," Sean says.

"You posed to be my nigga, and you out here fucking my bitch. Fuck the both of y'all," Adam says as starts pointing the gun toward Sean.

"Bro, be cool. She not even worth it. All of Richmond been ran through her, so if you gone kill us for fucking her, you gone have to kill half of Richmond," Sean says with his hands up.

"Bitch, you out here been fucking around on me?" Adam asks as he gets back on the phone with Keisha.

"Babe, they lying. Who you gone believe, your woman or them hating-ass niggas?" Keisha says.

"Man, if we lying then how we know she got a butterfly tattoo on her inner thigh?" Isaiah says.

"How the fuck they know that, Keisha?" Adam asks.

"Babe, I promise I ain't fucked on nobody else, just come over so we can talk 'bout it," Keisha says.

"Oh, bitch, we fasho gone talk 'bout this," Adam says as he turns away and walks away from the brothers.

Chapter 20

Night Night, Nigga

All of sudden, an all-black four-door Camry pulled up on Hartnet Court, and three niggas bounced out with ski masks on, catching Isaiah, Adam, and Sean all off guard.

"What's up, nigga? Run all that shit, bitch!" Sam says as he runs up on Isaiah and Sean with Dave.

"Yeah, bitch! Give me everything you got, nigga. You can come out them Jordans too, bitch!" Dave says.

"Yeah, nigga. I got your bitch ass now," I say as I point the gun at Adam.

"Nigga, who the fuck is you?" Adam asks as he puts his hands up and drops the phone.

"Nigga, I'm that nigga that's gone send you where you belong for what you did," I say.

"What I do, bro? What, I owe you money or something? Bro, I only got 250 on me. You can have that, just don't shoot me, bra," Adam says as he starts going for his gun in his waistband, acting as if he getting the money.

"Nigga, don't even try that shit. Put yo hands up, bitch," I say as I reach around and grab the gun from his waistband and put it behind my back.

Chapter 21

On the Floor

"Come on, bro, don't shoot me, man!" Adam says.

"Is that what my brother said before you shot him?" I asks.

"Your brother?" Adam asks.

"Yeah, nigga, my brother! You killed that nigga for nothing," I say.

"Michael?" Adam says as he turns around.

"Yeah, bitch nigga, it's me," I say as I take my mask off.

"Man, my bad for killing yo brother, bro. I didn't think the gun was loaded. I didn't know it was gone shoot like that," Adam says as he starts to cry.

"Bitch nigga, I don't want to hear that shit you shot my brother three times in his fucking face while them bitch-ass niggas was holding him. You looked me dead in my eyes and laughed," I say as I put the gun in his mouth, so he won't say another word.

"Maannn. Come on, man, kill that nigga," Sam says while pointing the gun at Sean and Dave pointing the gun at Isaiah.

"Man, shut up. I got this. I want this nigga to cry for his life, now that he know I own it," I say.

"Sam, is that you, nigga?" Isaiah asks.

"Yeah, bitch, it's me," Sam says.

"Nigga, how you gone do this to your own family?" Sam asks.

"Bitch, shut up. I said the same thing to y'all when that nigga robbed me just a couple of hours ago, and y'all ain't do shit," Sam says.

"Man, fuck all that talking. Let's hurry up before someone comes," Dave suggests.

"Aight, bro, aight."

"Nigga, you ready to see yo cousin Twan again? And tell my brother wassup, and I hope he beat yo ass in hell too," I say as I pull the trigger.

Click! Click! The gun misfires as Adam notices he quickly knocks the gun out of my hand and tackles me. We rumble on the floor, but Adam gets on top and throws multiple blows toward my head. I block them and push him off and get up, not knowing I pushed him right toward his gun that I put on the ground. He reaches for it and tries to grab it. I run around the car to take cover as he turns and starts shooting.

Boom! Boom!

Sean and Dave start to buss back at him as they start to also run for cover. That's when Isaiah and Sam get off the ground and try to run away and get out of the cross fire of bullets. They both run toward an alleyway, and Sam notices, so he starts to shoot their way.

"Aaaaaahhhhh," Isaiah says as he gets hit in the in the middle of his back.

"Bro, come on," Sean says as he notices that Isaiah is hit.

Pow! Boom! Pow!

Boom! Boom! Pow! Boom!

"Shit!" Adam says as he shoots his final bullets and tries to find a way out of the situation. He sees Sean and Isaiah limping away through the alley and knows he won't make it, so he tries to sneak around the house, and Michael notices so he runs after him, grabbing the gun that jammed on him. Just as Michael turns the corner to chase after him, he hears gunshots coming from in front of him.

Pow! Pow! Pow!

I turn around and see Lil Donny pointing the .22 at Adam with smoke coming from the barrel.

"That's for Bobby," Lil Donny says.

"D, man, what you doin'? You was posed to stay in the car," I say.

"Shit, I was till I seen y'all Niggas couldn't get the nigga, so I got out and did what y'all niggas couldn't. Straight up!" Donny says.

That's when Dave and Sam came running around the corner, noticing Adam's dead body as it lay in front of Lil Donny.

"Yo, what the fuck happen?" Dave asks.

"Nigga, what it look like? I got this nigga," Donny tells him.

"Damn, lil nigga, you was serious 'bout being ready, huh?" Sam asks.

"I been trying to tell Michael I been ready for this life," Lil Donny says with a grin.

"Man, I thought you was posed to kill this nigga Adam? What happened?" Dave asks me.

"Nigga, that weak-ass gun jammed on me when I was gonna blow that nigga brains out," I say.

"Man, let me see that," Sam says as he asks for the gun.

"Man, you had the shit on safety, my nigga," Sam says as he walks toward Adam's body.

Pow! Pow! Pow! Sam puts three more holes in Adam's chest.

"Damn, nigga, what you do that for?" I ask.

"Trust me, bro, I done seen niggas bounce back from a .22 shot. I had to make sure that nigga don't come back from the dead, and now you can say you killed him because this was your gun," Sam says.

"Man, hell naw! That ain't the same Lil Donny took that away from me, but as long as that bitch nigga dead, it's all good," I say.

"Well, we gotta go now because we did let them other niggas get away, and they saw y'all dumbasses' faces, so they probably calling people to come get us now," Dave says.

"Yeah, what's up with that shit? Y'all niggas was posed to handle them niggas while I took care of Adam," I say.

"Nigga, you didn't handle shit. Lil bro did that. You the one that froze up and let that nigga start bussing at us, you the real reason they got away," Dave says.

"Nigga, I ain't freeze up. That shit jammed on me," I say.

"Well, thank God lil bro was here because then Adam would've got away too," Sam says as he gives Lil Donny a high five.

"Man, fuck all that shit, let's go!" I say.

"Hold up!" Sam says as goes to Adam's body and goes through his pockets and gets the money and the weed that Adam stole from him.

"Nigga, what are you doing?" Dave says.

"Nigga, getting my shit back, what it look like?" Sam responds.

"Man, come on, we ain't got time for that shit," Dave says.

"A'ight, we gone," Sam says as he gets everything that was stolen from him back.

Chapter 22

The Ride Home

They all run around the corner to run back to the car just to see in a distance a yellow supreme Cutlass. Automatically, I notice that it was Uncle Stino in the car. The car burns rubber down the street as soon as he seen all our faces except for Dave's because he still has his mask on.

"Bro, who the fuck was that?" Sam asks.

"My uncle," Lil Donny says.

"Man, how he know where we was?" Sam asks.

"Shit how I'm posed to know?" I say as we all hop into the car.

"Fuck he saw our faces, y'all think he gone snitch on us?" Sam asks.

"Naw, he know better to put me behind bars. I know too much of his operation," I say.

"I hope you right, come on, Dave, get us the fuck up out here," Sam says.

"Nigga, what you think I'm trying to do? Shut the fuck up," Dave says as he starts the car and smashes down Hartnett Street, turning onto Carlson Street to hop right on the freeway.

"A'ight, where we goin'?" Sam asks.

"We gonna go back to where we got the car from and go back to my house," Dave says.

"Naw, get on the parkway, my uncle saw us in this car so he gone probably think we gone take it back there," I say.

"What's on the Richmond parkway?" Dave asks.

"Another one of his cars. We can leave this one there and take that one and then we gone go back to Dave house, so we can get our stories right on where we all was tonight," I explain.

We take the exit for the Richmond Parkway and pull into the p's, better known as North Richmond Projects. We pull up to a blue four-door Camry, and we all hop out to get in the other car and smash down to Dave's house.

"Bro! That was some hardcore shit. You pulled, lil bro, I didn't think you had it in you," Sam says.

"I told y'all I was ready for this shit. Now Bobby can rest in peace," Lil D says.

"Yeah, if it wasn't for you, Michael would've let that nigga get away," Dave says.

"Nigga, shut up. I was gone handle that nigga once I caught up to him," I say.

"Yeah, right, nigga," Dave says.

"It ain't like y'all did y'all part. Y'all let them other niggas get away, now we gotta worry 'bout them bussin' back at us," I say.

"Man, whatever, I'm ready for them niggas," Lil D says.

"Sit yo lil ass down. I'm gonna take yo ass home! Them niggas was right, I should've never brung your ass," I say.

"Don't get mad at little bro cause he handled your business for you. Shit, I'll rather ride out with that nigga than you. That was probably your first time handling a gun, huh?" Dave asks.

"Nigga, shut up! And so what? If it was, I ain't never had to use one on nobody," I say.

"I knew it. That's why you froze up," Dave says.

"Nigga, I didn't freeze up. That shit jammed on me. I should've just brung my gun like I was posed to," I say.

"Nigga, that shit ain't jam, you just froze just like you would've did with yo own shit," Dave says.

"Nigga, how many shots you got left?" I ask Dave.

"Nigga, my shit empty. I let all my shit out on them niggas. What the fuck you mean?" Dave says.

"And how many niggas you hit?" I ask.

"Nigga, none," Dave says as he now realizes where I'm going with it.

"Exactly, nigga! You shot your whole clip out and ain't hit shit. At least I gotta full clip," I say.

"Damn, bro. He is right. You ain't shit again, my nigga," Sam says as he starts laughing.

"Nigga, shut up with your cheerleading ass! Get off his dick," Dave says and everybody start laughing.

Dave pulls up to the house and tell everybody to get out.

"Nigga, you act like this your shit. Give me the keys," I say.

"Man, let me get this. Your uncle isn't gone even know I got it," Dave says.

"Nigga, please! Why would I give it to you when I'm 'bout to whip it around?" I say.

"Man, huh? Take the keys, this shit a bucket anyway," Dave says.

"Yeah, whatever, nigga, so let's get this shit straight now on where we was," I say before everybody get out the car.

"Shit, let's say we went to the movies or some shit," Lil Donny says.

"Where yo movie ticket at that shows you was there?" I say.

"Nigga, who keep movie tickets?" Dave asks.

"Nigga, what if the police go check the cameras out and don't see us on there going to the movies? That's our ass," I say.

"Okay. Okay, I see what you mean, so what we gone say?" Dave says.

"Well, first off y'all ain't seen me or Lil Donny from earlier when Bobby was shot. And Sam, you have never met us at all. Y'all niggas been at Dave house all day playing the game after you got jumped. Me and Lil Donny was at the park we usually go to when Donny get off school. I had to break the bad news to him, and we been there," I say.

"Damn, nigga! That's a pretty good idea. I see you like to use your head, huh?" Sam says.

"Naw, I just know how not to go to jail," I say.

"I can dig it. So it was nice not meeting you," Sam says.

"Real talk. I wanna thank y'all for riding for Bobby, man, I know he looking down on us right now proud that we got that nigga for him," I say.

"Especially you, lil bro," Dave says to Lil D.

"Aww! Look at who dick riding now," Sam says.

"Nigga, fuck you! He handled his shit today," Dave says.

"Naw you right, lil bro, down for the team," Sam says as he gives Lil D a handshake.

"Right on, y'all," Lil D says.

"A'ight, my niggas, y'all be cool," Sam says as he shakes Michael's hand and leaves the car to head into Dave's house.

Chapter 23

The Curse

"Bro, don't forget to wipe these off, so they can't come back to us," I say as I hand him back the gun I used.

"Ooh, yeah. Here you go," Lil D says as he tries to give the gun he killed Adam with.

"Naw, lil bro, you earned that, that's all you," Sam says.

"For real? Wow, bro! Thanks," Lil D says.

"Bro, don't give that nigga that he only ten years old," I say as I snatch the gun from him.

"Nigga, what you mean? That nigga handled his business with that gun. He got his first body with it, so it should be his," Sam suggests.

"Man, it's better the little nigga be strapped then caught slipping by these little niggas. stop being a bitch, bro," Dave says.

"Fuck you, nigga. I'll keep it for him cause y'all ain't gonna get my little brother killed by the police just cause this nigga think he big and bad with the gun on him," I say.

"A'ight, bro, you right, but I think little bro know better than to do dumb shit like that," Sam says.

"Well, I ain't gonna risk his life to find out. He is the only brother I have left, and I'll be damn if I lose him to this damn curse," I say.

"Nigga, what curse?" Dave ask.

"The curse of being raised in the hood environment that our parents passed down to us," I say.

"Nigga, I ain't cursed. What the fuck you talking 'bout?" Dave asks again.

"Oh yeah? What yo parents do for a living?" I ask.

"My mom's a nurse, and my dad's in jail," Dave answers.

"And how long yo daddy been in jail?" I ask.

"Nigga, I don't know. I don't fuck with that nigga ever since he left me and Moms and stop giving a fuck about us. It been fuck that nigga right back. All I know is the nigga went to jail when he was twenty-five," Dave says.

"See, right there is my proof you only have two ways to beat the curse and two ways to know you lose to the curse," I began to explain.

"Man, I don't want to hear that shit," Dave says.

"Man, shut up, I wanna hear this," Sam says.

"Man, come on, you believe this shit?" Dave asks.

"Believe it or not, nigga, I don't care. But the two ways you find out you failed the curse is when you locked up or dead before you turned twenty-six," I say.

"Nigga, what's the two ways to beat it then?" Sam asks.

"To become something in life out the hood or stay on top of the hood, but with staying on top of the hood you always have to fight to stay on top, or else you lose to the curse," I say.

"So the only way really to beat the curse is to become something out the hood?" Sam asks.

"Unless you ready to fight for the rest of your life," I say.

"Man, where the fuck you hear this dumb shit from?" Dave asks.

"My daddy told me two days before he got shot and killed at the age of twenty-six," I say.

"Damn, I guess he ain't beat the curse," Dave says.

"Come on, brah, that shit ain't funny," Sam says.

"Naw, it's good. Yeah, he didn't beat the curse, that's why I want different for Lil D because he may be the only one that can beat it out of our family. It may be too late for me and Bobby, but not him. I'll give my life for him to make it out," I say.

"You a real brother. I'll give you that, bro. I wish my brother could've thought like you when we was growing up," Sam says.

"Right on, bro," I say.

"Now who on who dick?" Dave says as he closes the door heading to his house.

"At least my last name ain't Dicksworth," Sam says as he finally closes the door.

"Nigga, fuck you," Dave says as he opens the door.

"A'ight, y'all. Y'all niggas be cool!" Lil D says, yelling out the window.

"A'ight, lil bro, till the next time," Dave says as he looks at Michael.

"A'ight, lil bro, don't mind his dumbass. Plug up the game so I could whoop yo ass in Madden right quick," Sam says.

"Nigga, he said act like we was playing Madden not actually play it," Dave says.

"Nigga, you just scared because I whooped on you last time," Sam says.

"Nigga, bet ten," Dave says as he enters the house.

"Nigga, bet," Sam says as he closes the door behind him.

Chapter 24

The Cleanup

We pull off and go home.

"So you know what we got to do when we go home, right?" I say as I head back home.

"What?" Lil D asks.

"As soon as we get home, we gotta wash and clean every part of our body and burn our clothes. So as soon as you undress put your clothes in the garbage bag under the sink," I say.

"What garbage bag? There ain't none under there, and I thought you said Mom didn't want you in the house," Lil D says.

"I put the bag in there before I left and prepared your other clothes in there too. And don't worry 'bout Mom, she probably knocked out drunk on the couch," I say.

"You think they gone catch me for killing him?" Lil D asks.

"I'll make sure no one will know you did anything, you hear me? I got you, Donny," I say.

"You think Bobby would've been proud of me?" Lil D asks.

"I know he is, Donny, I'm just sorry I brung you though. I should've left you," I say.

"Why not? If I wasn't there, he would've got away," Lil D says.

"I'd rather him getting away then scarring you for life with taking someone life," I say.

"It ain't that bad," Lil D admits.

"Yeah. For now, lil bro, taking someone's life is a life changer. Knowing you killed someone is going to haunt you forever, but I'll be here for you whenever you need me to talk to," I say.

"Aight, bro, but can I ask you something?" Lil D says.

"What's up?" I say as I turn on Sanford, the street that we live on, and park the car a couple houses down from the house.

"How you know what happens to a person when they kill someone when you said you ain't never killed no one?" Lil D says.

"You probably don't remember because you were a baby at the time, but once when I was six years old someone tried to rob us. It was me and Bobby in our room playing the game and you in the crib with mama in the living room, and all of a sudden a guy comes bussing through the door with a gun, asking where is the money and the drugs. Mama tells him there isn't any and that he has the wrong house. He slaps her across the face, and she flies across the room. Me and Bobby hear the scuffle and peek out our bedroom door to see what's going on. We see Mama laid down on the floor and your crib knocked over. Bobby runs to Mommy and Daddy room and grab Daddy's gun out the closet where Daddy told us it would be if anything go wrong. We were to use it and protect this family. So Bobby got it and ran down the hallway and pointed the gun at him. The guy was flipping over the couch cushions and tearing up the living room looking for the stash until he turned around and seen Bobby pointing the gun at him."

What you gone do with that, lil nigga? You ain't no shooter," the guys says with drunken slur.

"You better leave us alone, or I'ma bust one in yo ass," Bobby says.

I run up behind Bobby. "Bobby man, what you doing?" I say.

"What it look like, nigga? I'm protecting this family. Now put yo hands up, bitch, don't try none of that slick shit," Bobby says.

Baby crying: "Whhaaaa! Whaaaa! Whhaa!"

"Man, you pushed my little brother on the floor? Now I must definitely got to kill you," Bobby says.

"You not gone kill me, young blood," the guy says with a smile.

"Oh yeah?" Bobby says as he cocks back the gun.

"Yeah, because I can see it in your eyes that you don't have it in you to take my life," the guy says, taking a step closer to us.

"Don't move another step, or I'll shoot," Bobby says.

"No, you won't. I don't think you're ready for the nightmares I'll be giving you," the man says.

"What nightmares?" Bobby asks.

"The nightmares of my soul being attached to yours, forever. Everywhere you go, I'll be there. Any time you think I'll be there, anytime you think you are going to be happy, I'll take it away from you just like you took my life away from me. I will haunt you forever," the guy says as he gets closer.

Bobby just freezes up, trembling in fear. His hands are so shaky that he accidently drops the gun. The guy makes his way toward us, pushing everything over to get to us. I hurry up and pick up the gun and close my eyes and shoot. *Pow!* It hits him right between his eyes, and he falls face first toward us. I stand in shock as I don't believe what just happened.

"Man, what you do that for? I had that nigga," Bobby says as he pushes me.

"Man, you froze up. What you think I was gone let him do, just kill us?" I say.

"Man, whatever. You think he dead?" Bobby says as he walks toward the body and kicks him.

"Man, don't do that," I say.

"Damn, nigga, you smoked his ass," Bobby says as he realizes he is dead.

"Man, shut up and pick Donny up, and I'll check on Mama," I say.

"So wait a minute. You mean to tell me you the one that shot that nigga instead of Bobby?" Lil D says.

"Yeah, that's how I know it can haunt you because that man haunts me till this day," I say.

"So I was doing his homework and cleaning up his room for nothing?" Lil D says.

"Who?" I ask.

"Bobby that nigga would always tell me that story to make me feel bad and do something for him because he said he was the one who killed him and saved my life," Lil D says.

"Naw, lil bro, it was me. He was just using you," I say as I start laughing.

"That shit ain't funny. That nigga room was nasty as shit. Now I'ma beat his ass," Lil D says then remembers that Bobby is dead and starts to cry.

"I know, lil bro, it hurts, trust me. I know. But Bobby in a better place right now looking down on us proud that we did not let his killer get away. So be strong and just know I'ma always be here to protect you no matter what. You hear me?" I say as I reach over and give Lil D a hug.

"Yes, I'm gon miss him though, man," Lil D says.

"I know, lil bro, I'm gone miss him too," I say.

"Come on, let's go inside, and remember I need you to really wash your body clean and brush and scrub under your nails with the peroxide on top of the counter. I left that there so we won't leave no evidence behind, so nothing will be traced to us," I explain as we exit the car.

"Okay, bro, but how you know all these things on how to get away with murders?" Lil D asks.

"Because Daddy came home plenty of nights with blood all over him, and one night he caught me peeking in to see what was going on at that moment. Daddy told me all 'bout the game of the hood, and that's when he also told me about the curse of the hood and how he wanted us to be the ones to beat the generational curse," I say.

"So do you think we can beat it?" Lil D asks.

"Not for me, D, but I'll spend the rest of my days making sure you do. That's why I need you to stay headstrong in class and become the doctor you always talking about you are," I say.

Lil D starts to laugh.

"What's so funny? I'm dead as serious 'bout this, Donny, I need you to believe in you just as much as I do," I say.

"Naw, bro, I know you are. When you said that doctor stuff, it reminded me of Bobby blaming me for everything he did in the house and yelling doctor D did it. That shit used to make me hella mad," Lil D says and smiles.

"Yeah, he was something else, man. Look after us, Bobby," I say as I look into the sky and cross my chest and send a kiss to the sky.

CHAPTER 25

REMEMBERING BOBBY

We walk into the house. As I predicted, Eve is knocked out with her wig sideways, a cigarette still lit in one hand and a half-tilted glass drink of taka vodka.

"What I tell you, lil bro?" I say, laughing out loud, shaking my head.

"Bro. Damn, is she alive?" Lil D asks as I take the glass out her hand softly. Eve starts to move and murmur.

"David, move now, leave me alone"

I then I grab the lit cigarette out the other hand and put it out in the ashtray and go pour out the drink in the sink.

"Now go straight to the bathroom and do what I said to do," I tell Donny.

"Okay, bro," Lil D says as he heads to the main bathroom, and I go to mama's bathroom and do the same thing Lil D was told to do.

After I get out the shower and done with scrubbing my hand's fingernails, I brush my teeth. I put the clothes I had on in the bag under the sink. As I'm done with that, I look up in the mirror and see Adam right beside me. I turn quickly and notice no one was there but me. I turn back to the mirror, only to see my reflection. I put my head in the sink to put water over my face. When I'm done, I grab a towel to dry it, and this time looking in the mirror I see the guy I killed when I was six years old. He was in the mirror right next to me just as Adam was. I look again just to find out I'm yet all alone. I look back at the mirror and now have Adam on one side of me while the other man is on the other. I look at them and say to myself. "This shit ain't real, it's all in my head."

I dip my head under the water once again, thinking that it would make them go away. I grab the towel and dry my face slowly, this time peeking through to look at the mirror and to find Bobby smiling at me. This time I don't look away. "Bobby, it's you!" I say as I start crying.

"Yeah, it's me, bitch. Why you always crying?" Bobby says.

"Nigga, fuck you," I say as I start smiling and wiping away my tears.

"This shit ain't even real, but I miss you, bro," I say.

"I miss you too, bro," Bobby says as he puts his hands on my shoulder, and I actually feel it.

"What the fuck?" I jump as I really feel his touch and can actually see him standing right next to me.

"Nigga, I know we brothers and all, but nigga can you put some clothes on? I ain't tryna see all that," Bobby says.

"How is this possible? Your pose to be dead," I say.

"It's a long story," Bobby says.

"Well, nigga, you should have plenty of time to tell me. You know, seeing how you're dead," I say.

"Ooohh, look who became a comedian. That was a horrible death joke by the way," Bobby says.

"Bobby, what are you doing here?" I say.

"Well, I can't tell you everything, but big man says I can tell you a little bit," Bobby says.

"Tell me what?" I say.

"How when we die, our souls are stuck until we get justice for our lives we past lived, and y'all did that for me, and now my soul is free to walk

the earth as I please," Bobby says.

"That's great, man, let's go tell Mama. She gone love this," I say.

"It ain't that easy, bro, the only people who can see me is the ones who saw me when I died," Bobby explains.

"Why the ones who saw you when you died can only see you?" I ask.

"Don't ask me, the man upstairs makes the rules, and we just gotta follow them," Bobby says.

"So why are you here when you can be anywhere else?" I ask.

"Because I spoke to dad, and he told me to come back and help y'all beat this curse," Bobby says.

"You spoke to dad? How is he? Where is he?" I ask.

"His soul is still stuck," Bobby says truthfully.

"How is that possible? I thought they got the person who killed him," I say.

"Turns out, they didn't get all of them," Bobby says.

"Did he tell you who else it was?" I say.

"Naw, he didn't tell me much or at least he wouldn't let him tell me," Bobby says.

"Who is *him*?" I say.

"God, dumbass!"

"Oohhh," Bobby says as he jumps like he been shocked and looks up.

"What was that?" I say.

"This nig… Oohhh, a'ight, man, I'll stop. It's our heavenly father telling me to watch my mouth. You happy?" Bobby says as he looks up.

"Man, this shit is really real," I say.

"Yeah, nig… I mean, yeah, man, this is real," Bobby says.

"But how the hell you make it to heaven with all the bad shit you used to do?" I ask.

"That's a question I ask myself, bro, but all I know once them niggas had my arms while I was on my knees and saw you running toward me, I started praying to God," Bobby says.

"I thought you didn't believe in God," I say.

"I didn't. Until that moment, he has made a believer out of me," Bobby says.

"So have you met him?" I ask.

"Naw, no one has. He just a bright light that speaks into our minds and tells us what to do," Bobby says.

"So what are you sent here to do?" I say.

"I don't know for sure, but he told me I had to come back to finish it," Bobby says.

"Finish what? We got the one who killed you," I say.

"Like I said, I don't know, maybe it's for getting justice for dad and finally letting him free," Bobby says.

"How we posed to find out who killed him? That shit happened a long time ago," I say as I put the last of my clothes on and head out of Mom's bathroom and check to see if she was still knocked out. I notice her body shaking, so I grab a cover and place it over her body, softly so I don't wake her up. But she turns and open her eyes and says, "David, why you didn't just go with plans? Why you let them kill you and leave me with these nappy-headed niggas? You wanted this family, not me," she says as she gets cozy with the blanket and falls back to sleep.

I stand there looking at her, not believing the words that just came out her mouth.

"Did you just hear that?" I ask as I look back at Bobby, but he wasn't there. "Bobby? Bobby?" I yell, going back to Mama's bathroom just to find out he's not there either. That's when I notice his bedroom door slightly open. "Bobby, you in here?" I ask.

"Man, I'm gon miss this room," Bobby says, looking around his room, having memories flash through his mind of how it use to be when he was alive.

"Yeah, I think you the only one gone miss it," I say as I close the door.

"What you mean? You ain't gone miss me?" Bobby asks.

"Naw, nigga, I am but your room, naw I ain't gon miss it. You know your shit was always dirty and stanky," I say.

"Man, whatever, my room was designed just for me, so I can know where all my shit is. That's why you could never find my stash." Bobby smiles as he smells his room, taking in a big breath.

"Nigga, you mean your stash under your bed under the broken wood on the floor?" I say as I laugh.

"Nigga, how'd you know it was there? I thought you never found it when I betted you my whole stash to your twenty dollars that you couldn't find it," Bobby says.

"Please, nigga, you forgot I had the room first. I knew about that floor," I say as I laugh.

"Nigga, then why you give me the twenty dollars? That was dumb to do," Bobby says. "Whoever said it was my twenty dollars? I paid you with your own money, I grabbed it out of your stash," I say.

"I knew I wasn't tripping about my money being short all the time," Bobby says.

"Please! Nigga, I had my own money. I didn't need yours. I only took that twenty from you, but hey I gave it back," I say as I start cracking up.

"Then who else could've took it? You the only one who knew where it was?" Bobby asks.

"Nigga, I don't know," I say as I start to walk over to his bed and go to his stash spot.

"What are you doing, man?" Bobby asks.

"Nigga, taking your stash before mamma come in here and start ransacking this room, unless you want to take it with you to heaven," I say in a sarcastic way. "Nigga, so you gone rob me right in front of me? You couldn't wait until I left? You a cold-ass nigga," Bobby says.

"Nigga, shut up!" I say as take out his money.

"Where you get this gun from?" I ask as I pull out a revolver.

"Dad gave me that before he died, he said I was supposed to take care of the family and protect y'all," Bobby says.

"Yeah, a lot of good you did," I say as I laugh.

"What the fuck! Ooowwww!" Bobby says as he looks up.

"What you mean by that?" Bobby says.

"I mean, how you gone protect us when you're dead, and I was the one protecting your dumb ass when you was alive. You never knew how to grow up," I say.

"Nobody asked you to do nothing for me. I never asked for help," Bobby says.

"Yes, because Dad gave me that same lame as speech before he died, that's why I always helped you when you never asked for it," I say.

"Nigga, where was you at then? When the niggas smoked me?" Bobby asks.

"God, if you don't sound like Mama. If you didn't run your mouth 'bout Twan like I told you not to, you would still be here. I tried my best to get there to protect you, but I was too late.

"I'm sorry, Bobby," I say as I sit on Bobby's bed. "Naw, you right. I messed up, bro, I should've been smarter like you. I let that money get to my head, and now it got me dead," Bobby says as he sits next to me.

"But I'm gone help you beat this curse for you and Lil D too. How is he by the way?" Bobby asks.

"He took your death pretty hard, shit we all did, but he proved that he was ready for this life by killing Adam," I say.

"What the fuck. Oooowwwwwww!"

"Look if you gone be doing that every time I cuss, then you might as well send me to hell," Bobby says, looking up.

"Who are you talking to?" I say.

"God! Man, every time I cuss he do this thing that shocks the hell out of my body, and I he think it's funny," Bobby says.

"So he listening to us right now?" I ask.

"Man, he sees all and knows all. Everything you thinking right now, he knows he has created our future and past," Bobby says.

"So what's in my future then?" I ask.

"Nigga, I don't know I said. He see that shiiii… I mean, he see it, not me," Bobby says as he catches himself from cussing.

"But anyway, what you mean Lil D killed Adam? I thought Uncle Stino did," Bobby says.

"Naw, fuck that nigga," I say.

"Oh, but you let this nigga say whatever he want, where his shock at?" Bobby says, raising his hands and looking up.

"Why you ain't messing with Unc?" Bobby asks.

"Man, he was acting like I wasn't ready to get revenge for your death," I say.

"No offense, bro, I would have thought the same thing. You not the killing type of person," Bobby says.

"Nigga, what you mean? I caught that nigga slipping. I ran up right behind him while he was on the phone with the barrel on the back of his head, ready to blow his brains out," I explain.

"Then how Lil D killed him?" Bobby asks.

"Because the piece-of-shit gun Dave talked me into using jammed on me, and he got away and we had a big-ass shootout," I say.

"Wait, my nigga Dave was there?" Bobby says.

"Yeah, and Sam was too. The niggas that was holding you was Sam cousins," I say.

"Damn, my niggas rolled out for me? That's wassup," Bobby says.

"Yeah, but we let them other niggas get away. Sam got one of them in the back when they ran off, though," I say.

"So that nigga Dave ain't hit shit again? Hahahaah! Ooowwww," Bobby says, looking up.

"What you mean again?" I ask.

"Nothing, man, so y'all gone get the rest of them niggas too, right?" Bobby tries to whisper.

"Yeah, man, don't worry they gone get theirs, and the nigga who gave the hit out on you," I say.

"What you mean hit?" Bobby asks.

"The nigga you knocked out told me some nigga named Nitz-O told them everything about us, and that's how Adam knew how to find us," I say.

"Who is Nitz-O?" Bobby asks.

"I don't know, but I'm gone find out, and he gone get his," I say as the door creaks open.

"Bro! Who you talking to?" Lil D comes in and asks.

I look around and don't see Bobby anywhere and start to feel like I'm crazy. "Uumm, nobody, I guess bro just in here remembering Bobby. You all cleaned up?" I say.

"Yeah, my clothes in the garbage bag by the door in the hall-way," Lil D says. "Good to hear you did real good tonight, lil bro.

I know for sure Bobby would've been proud 'bout what you did tonight," I say.

"Thanks, bro, you think he in heaven?" Lil D asks. I know he's at peace, and I don't know if heaven ready for him yet, lil bro," I say as I laugh.

"Yeah. He was a wild one, huh? I'ma miss him," Lil D says as he goes to Bobby's pictures on the wall of him and his brothers and a magazine poster of Megan Good.

"Remember how he was always saying he gone marry Megan Good?" Lil D says as he points to the poster.

"Yeah, damn near cried for a week to Mama when I took it off the wall and hid it from him," I say as we laugh.

"Man, I remember when he betted me twenty dollars if I couldn't find his stash spot," Lil D says.

"Did you ever find it?" I ask.

"Naw, not when he betted me. I lost the twenty, but the next day he went to his stash, and he forgot to close his door all the way, so I saw where it was. So I went to go get my twenty and a couple extra as soon as he left," Lil D says, laughing out loud.

"I knew I wasn't the only one going in there," I say.

"So have you checked it?" Lil D asks.

"Yeah, it looks like Mama knew where it was too because it was empty," I say.

"Damn! How you think Mama gone feel after she finds out we got the nigga that killed Bobby?" Lil D asks.

"I don't know because she not gone find out we did," I say.

"Why not?"

"Because we don't know if we can trust her right now," I say.

"Come on, man, it's Mama," Lil D says.

"I'm serious, bro, she can never know we did this, or she is going to hold this over our head forever. Do you understand it's only us now, and we got to take care of each other?" I say.

"Okay," Lil D says.

"Man, I'ma miss you," I say as I look at a picture of Bobby in my hand.

"I'm gone miss him too, bro," Lil D says as he comes and sits by me and starts to cry and lets a tear drop fall on the face of Bobby's picture.

Chapter 26

Rest in Peace, Bobby

"Earlier today I laid to rest yet another victim to the streets of Richmond. A young black male and yet again these streets said no, that's not enough, I want more. See, the devil loves the hood, it is his playground, a place where he doesn't have to do anything. He just sits back and let us make it easier for him to control us," Pastor Sergio says.

The crowd agrees with him, saying amen.

"Today we are not saying goodbye to young Bobby, today we are saying, 'See you in the next life.' See, we can't mourn for him right now. We have to be joyful because Bobby has taking steps closer to the everlasting life. Can I get an amen?" Pastor Sergio says.

"Amen," the crowd responds.

"You see, we all just stuck in the now, but once you get to that everlasting life there's no more pain, no more being broke, no more killing of young black men, no more parents burying their kids. I tell y'all, there is another life past death, and that young man is closer than we are, so if you want to mourn something, mourn how we are still stuck in the now. Mourn how we still got to bury our kids now. Mourn how the hood ain't gone never change, it's always going to devour our youth, and we can't do nothing about it but just wait till we get to where Bobby is, so if you feeling sad for Bobby, don't be. You should be feeling happy because he will be forever looking down on us. He will be protecting those who loved him from above, making sure our now living will prepare us for the afterlife," Pastor Sergio says.

"At this moment, I want to ask that we take a moment of silence to say our last words to Bobby like he was sitting right next to you at this very moment. What would you tell him? I want everyone to close they eyes and bow their head and talk to him," Pastor Sergio says. Everyone in the crowd follows the pastor's instructions.

"Oooooo god! Why they had to take my baby?" Eve bursts out and yells in the front row of the church.

"Not my baby, Bobby, why you had to leave me down here with these demons?" she takes her glasses off and say.

"Eve! Don't you start that shit in here," Stino says.

"Fuck you, Stino! That's my Boy right there! I can say whatever the fuck I want!" Eve yells back at Stino.

"Mama, come on now, please," I say.

"Boy, shut up! You should've been saying please to them niggas that killed my baby," Eve says as she stands up and points to Bobby's body.

"Eve! Sit down and let us put this boy to rest," Dave's mom says.

"Bitch, ain't nobody even talkin' to yo ass. That ain't yo boy up there, is it?" Eve continues to yell.

"No it ain't, but you do have two other boys right here next to you who also needs you to be the mother that you need to be," Monica says.

"Bitch, I know you ain't given me advice on being a mother. Dave don't even know who the fuck his father is, and you don't even know how to keep a man," Eve says loud enough for the whole service to hear.

"Eve, sit yo ass down and shut up. Damn, you always got to ruin something," Stino says.

"Fuck you, Stino! You the reason my son laying there dead now. All Bobby wanted to do was follow in yo footsteps! All he wanted was to be like you, a drug dealer, a killer. You gone burn in hell for what you did," Eve says.

"Bitch, you need to sit yo drunk ass down and shut the fuck up. If it wasn't for me, your kids would've been in the fucking system, and yo drunk ass would've been dead or doped up somewhere in a bando, not giving two fucks about them kids, just like you do now," Stino stands up and says.

"It's bad enough you took my kids' fathers away, but now you want my boys too? Damn! What you want me all to yourself? Here I am, just leave my boys be," Eve says.

"Bitch, don't nobody want yo dopefien'-looking ass. Gone you need to shut the fuck up. You don't know what you talking about," Stino says.

"Naw, I know what the fuck I'm talking about," Eve says.

"Brothers and sisters, please let's stop this. You see how the devil works. It turns us against each other. We're posed to be here rejoicing over sending Bobby home to the almighty Lord himself, now stop this fighting and let us all remember the good times we had with Bobby," the pastor interrupts Eve and says as he gives a signal to the choir to start singing.

"God, come in your house today, fill us with peace and joy. Please get rid of the devil, works from this place, may you bless every single person in this room. Fill us with your holy spirit. I know we lost another child, but you needed him more than we did God. We believe in your word, and you say that through you we can do anything. I pray young Bobby had no more suffering, no pain, as he transfers over to you, Lord. We know you raise us to fulfill a purpose in life, and I pray that Bobby has done his. I pray that it brings his family together more than ever, Lord. Put your mighty hands on this family, may each person grow into the person you called them to be. May each one of them fulfill their purpose because, Lord Jesus, they cannot afford to lose anyone else. I ask that you break the curse on this family," Pastor says.

"Amen," the crowd says as everyone stands and yells.

"Now I didn't know young Bobby that well," Pastor says.

"Not many in here did," Eve says.

"Sister Eve, come on now," Pastor says.

"Sorry, Pastor," Eve says as she sits down.

"As I was saying, I didn't know young Bobby, but hearing what my young daughter told me he had a very good sense of humor. At this moment I would like to ask his brother Michael to come up here and tell us more about him."

"Come on up here, son," Pastor says as he puts me on the spot.

I look around to Mama.

"Nigga go up there, what you looking at me for?" Eve says.

I get up, shaking my head. I walk up the stairs to the podium lower the microphone to my height.

Screeeech! The microphone lets out a loud noise.

"Sorry! Umm, I don't know what to say," I say.

"Speak from your heart, son, tell us. Matter of fact, tell Bobby how much you loved him," Pastor says.

I look at the podium then look into the back of the crowd to notice all the people staring at me. I start to get nervous.

"Man, you 'bout to cry, huh?" Bobby asks.

I quickly look up and see Bobby sitting in my seat next to Mama. I wipe my eyes as if they was playing tricks on me, and yet there Bobby is smiling.

"Come on, man, tell me how much you love me," Bobby says, smiling.

I shake my head and start smiling.

"My brother Bobby was an asshole!" I say.

The crowd murmurs around, gasping for air.

"But he was my asshole! He always got on my nerves, but at the end of the day he was my brother. I couldn't ever stay mad at him for too long. He always knew how to talk his way out of getting in trouble. I remember the day Bobby talked Mama out of whooping him," I say as the crowds laugh.

"It was an Easter Sunday, and we were all in our white church clothes, and Bobby decides to go outside he finds a stray dog outside of the house. He picks him and brings him in saying, 'Aye, y'all look what I found outside, I'ma name it Raider.' I tell him to put the dog down and take it back where he got it from, you don't know what the dog has, so he puts it down, and his white suit is covered in dirt. I tell him Mama gonna kill him for getting it dirty, he kicks the dog in anger, trying to blame him. Mama comes in the room after putting on her earrings and notice how dirty Bobby is and the dog in the room. She takes her earrings right back off. 'Bobby, what the hell did you do?' He tells Mama that God sent the dog to our doorstep to make us a family again. She tells me to go get the belt out of her room. I run and go get it and Bobby runs right behind me. Mama yells, 'Boy, you bet not run from me, it's only gone be worse.' Bobby pushes me out the way and runs into Mama's room and locking it behind him, Mama tries to open the door, but she can't get in. 'Bobby, open this damn door now.' 'Hell naw," Bobby says, you just whooped me two days ago, my ass still don't feel right since then. I like to sit down, Mama, he says.'"

"Boy, I'm not playing with you. You got until five seconds to open this door, or else," Mama says.

"Or else what, huh, Mama? You already threatening me with a whooping. What's worser then that?" he yells back.

"Boy, open this door, or I'ma break this door," Mama says.

"Mama, I know we don't have insurance, so if you break it, that mean the landlords gone ask what happened, and I'ma tell them you beat the shit out of me, and that's gone involve cops now. Come on, Mama, you know you don't want that, do you?" he says.

Mama tries to wiggle the doorknob and bangs on the door. "Get your scrawny little ass out here now, Bobby," Mama yells.

"No, Mama! Why would you want to whoop me anyway? I was doing a good thing given a dog a home, what do you think Jesus would say right now?"

"Jesus can't give me the money I paid for that suit, so he can't tell me shit," Mama says as she still tries to open the door.

"Mama, we got this suit at fallas yesterday, and you only spent twenty on it."

"Boy, do you got twenty dollars to give me?"

"Matter of fact, yes I do and it's all yours if you don't whoop me."

"Where the hell you get money from?"

"Do you want the money or not, Mama?"

"Where is it at boy?"

"Naw, you got to promise me you ain't gone whoop me."

"Boy, you better tell me before I change my mind."

"Okay, it's in my drawer with my draws in it."

Mama went in his room and went to the drawer where he said his money was and saw that it was five hundred dollars in there, and she grabbed 250 dollars and told me and Donny as well as Bobby to go take off our clothes, and she will be back later and ran out the house as if it were on fire.

"Hold up, you stole the money I gave to Lil Bobby?" Stino says, interrupting me.

"I sure did. He was ten years old. What he gone do with five hundred dollars? I needed that money more than he did," Eve says.

"Bitch, you probably just went to go get high or drunk. Matter of fact, ain't that the day you was caught in Jerrys bathroom sucking a nigga dick?" Stino asks.

"Fuck you, nigga, you just mad because it wasn't you," Eve says.

"Brothers and sisters, please not in the house of the Lord," Pastor says.

"Man, can y'all stop? My fucking brother is right here dead, and that's all y'all can do is talk about money and who fucked who. Y'all both are the reason he dead right now! Stino, you took care of us and all, but you also showed us a life we can never win in, where we would always be fighting for our lives instead of living it the best way we can out of the hood. And Mama, you never loved us, you only loved what we can do for you. If it's not beneficial to you, then it really is irrelevant to you. I just hope Bobby's death shows you how much of a mother you was to us because we are the mirror image of our parents, and what you teach us is the way we will grow into. I just hate that my brother had to pay the price for your failures, but I will not let you do that to Donny. I refuse to let him fall into this stupid curse that y'all set over our lives!" I yell into the microphone as I started crying.

"Now this is a true act of God right here, and it just takes one generation to change a generation. Now if this child of God can speak the future over his brother's life and confess the curse be broken in their lives, what makes you think God is not real? The devil attacks our youth because he knows they can destroy his future. He uses them as weapons to kill each other because he knows that they are God's weapons to destroy him, but us as parents have to lead them into the right direction so that the devil has no effect on our children. Once becoming a parent, you assume that you are protector of your child, but what the devil doesn't want you to know is that you're protecting God's weapons. See, he works in mysterious ways that no one can figure out, but he has a plan for each and every last one of us. You may not believe it, brothers and sisters, but we all have a purpose on this earth. You may not have found yours and wonder what it is. I ask you to talk to the father above know his word find the right path that he created for you, and let him lead you down it. We have to let ourselves stop living for ourselves and live for God. Let him be your provider, your protector, and your heavenly father," Pastor says as puts his arms around me.

The crowd screams amen and starts clapping.

"Now, heavenly father, I ask that you move through your house, Lord, touch each and every person in your sanctuary. Be blessed with this unwanted curse lifted off of their lives."

"Yessss!" the crowd murmurs.

"I ask that you open each and every one of our eyes and mind, Lord Jesus, let us find the path that you created for us. Let the purpose of our lives bring back the dreams of becoming something in life, Lord Jesus. I pray that you keep showing your love and mercy over your children, and Lord Jesus, let each and every parent know now, Lord Jesus, that we are not only protecting your weapons but that we are also preparing them for the war against the devil's work. Let Brother Bobby be the end of this wicked curse over this family. I pray that you let these young men be healed of their broken hearts over the loss of their flesh and blood, but Lord Jesus, let them be strengthened by your almighty power. I ask that Lord Jesus may this family grow into the empire it was always supposed to be. Let this family flourish with blessings, Lord Jesus.

"Oh Jessuusss! I feel you in this house today," the crowd says "amen" as they start standing, and some start speaking in tongues with hands in the air, catching the Holy Ghost.

"Lord Jesus, we give you your weapon back to you on this day because we did not know how to use him. Lord Jesus, we ask that you meet our young brother Bobby at the holy gates with open arms. Lord Jesus, may his death ignite the fire in this family that has been lowered by the devil for so long. We ask that you break the curse, Lord Jesus," Pastor says as he lifts his hand toward Eve's way. Eve rolls her eyes and looks around at everybody, noticing the ones catching the Holy Ghost and speaking in tongues.

Chapter 27

A Soul Confession

As we all gather around the casket of Bobby at Rolling Hills Memorial graveyard, just about to lower his body in the dirt, six feet down.

"Is there anyone that wants to say any final words as we lay young Bobby to rest?" Pastor asks.

"Yes, I would like to say a few words," Stino announces.

"Aww, hell naw! You not gonna speak shit over my baby!" Eve yells out.

"Sister Eve, please let him talk. Come on here, brother, and speak your mind," Pastor says.

"Thank you, Pastor," Stino says as he gives a mug to Eve.

"Well, as you all know David was like my brother, we done a lot of shit growing up, and he would always have my back so once he died his boys became my boys," Stino goes on to say.

"Huuh." Eve rolls her eyes and says.

"Anyway, like I was saying, these boys needed a man in their life to teach them how to be a man. Although David did his best when he was here, like young Bobby, he was taken too early," Stino says.

"Yeah, because you took both of them from me," Eve says.

"Woman! I ain't had nothing to do with this! I loved little Bobby like he was my own. That Lil Nigga had a bright future just like his daddy, which I had nothing to do with it either. So if you want to blame anybody, bitch, blame yourself because that's your son right there that I'm burying for you. You wouldn't have shit, Eve, if I haven't been here to take care of you and these lil niggas. And I did all I can to raise them, but we both know they was never mine to take care of in the first place, but I did that out of my respect for David.

That was my nigga, and he would've done the same for me if it was me gone, that's why in honor of my nigga David I got it arranged to where Bobby will be laid right next to his Dad," Stino says, pointing at David's headstone on the right reading: "Rest in paradise Big D sun rise January: 9th, 1976 sunset: January 9th, 2002."

Everyone starts to look, not even recognizing that David's grave site was right next to them this whole time they were there. Eve took off her glasses in shock because she hasn't been to David's grave site since they laid him to rest, so she starts crying.

"I just know that Bobby will not die in vain. I'ma make sure all the rest of the people that had something to do with the death of my lil nigga will pay," Stino says as he starts looking at me.

"Now, now, brother Stino, vengeance is not the way to seek justice. The Lord will deal with these murderers that killed young Bobby. If we take it into our own hands, we are only doing the devil's work. Let the Lord be the punisher on these lost souls of this generation," Pastor says.

"Well, the Lord better catch those niggas before I do, because vengeance is mine to serve to them niggas for taking my lil nigga," Stino says, walking back to his spot so they can now lay Bobby to rest.

"All right, brother and sisters, it's that time now that we send young Bobby here home to our heavenly father. We celebrate this day, not as death, but as a rebirth. Young Bobby impacted a lot of our lives, and we will cherish every memory we had with him, and we will forever remember your smile. Let your smile forever brighten up our day when we think of you."

As the groundsman starts lowering Bobby into the dirt, I walk up to the casket and kiss it and whisper to it, "Until next time, baby bro," and lay a white flower on top of the casket and then walk to my dad's headstone and kiss it also and whisper to it, "I'm sorry, Pop, I failed you. I couldn't protect the family, but I will now, and I promise ain't nobody gone hurt us no more," I say as I start crying.

Stino comes and holds me as he starts crying too, telling me, "It's gone be okay, lil nigga."

I start crying even more in his arms, not having no control over my emotions, feeling nothing but hurt and pain like a part of my soul has been torn out as they lower him all the way down in the dirt six feet deep.

Eve walks up, taking her glasses off to throw her white flower in the dirt and blows a kiss at Bobby's casket. As she gets done doing that, she looks up to David's headstone. She can barely stand the sight of it because of feeling guilty for not coming to see him all these years and puts her glasses back on as she turns around and goes back to her seat, then everyone who had a flower started tossing them into the grave-site hole. Even Keisha came up to toss a rose in. Before she goes back to her seat, she goes to Eve and sends her condolences.

"I'm so sorry for your loss," she says and gives Eve a hug. As she walks back, she looks at me with a look of nervousness. Seeing how emotional I was, she just goes to her seat without saying nothing. Mary goes up too and tosses her flower into the pit and rushes over to me to check on me.

"I know, Michael, it hurts but you are going to be okay. I'm here for you," Mary says.

As Stino recognizes who she is, he quickly stops hugging me and walks away like he has seen a ghost. I then turn to Mary as she starts to comfort me as everyone is saying their final goodbyes to Bobby. The groundskeepers start shoveling the dirt on top of his casket. A lot of people start to cry, showing all the love they had for Bobby with tears as they scoop the final dirt on to his grave site. People start to leave and start heading to the repass, gathering at the Richmond city hall where Stino made reservations at.

"Michael, let's go, boy you know I hate this damn place, it gives me the creeps," Eve says.

"I'ma stay here for a little while longer," I say.

"Boy, if you don't bring yo ass on, I'm not coming back up here to come get yo ass! So let's go," Eve says.

"Mrs. Eve, it's okay, I'll make sure I get him home," Mary says.

"And who are you?" Eve asks.

119

"It's me, Mary. Michael's best friend," Mary explains.

"Ain't you Rebecca baby girl?" Eve asks.

"Yes, ma'am, I am," Mary says.

"Well, since I ain't seen her in I don't know how long, tell her I ain't forgot about that twenty dollars she owe me. I'ma still need that, and boy don't be out here all night, we got to clean Bobby's room up. We got a CPS inspection on Wednesday, and I don't need them finding nothing, so take yo ass home and clean it up. I'ma be at Jerry's for a little while if you need me," Eve says as I just sit there, not acknowledging her.

"I'll make sure he gets home safely, Mrs. Eve," Mary says.

"Uummhmmm, I bet you will," Eve says as she takes her glasses off her to look at Mary and puts them back on and walks away.

"Don't forget about your little brother. Since you man enough to take care of him, he is yo responsibility," Eve says, waving her hand bye.

"Man, yo mama is something else," Mary says.

"I can't stand that bitch, she gets on my damn nerves," I say.

"Don't say that about your mother, no matter what y'all go through, that is still your mother," Mary says.

"As soon as she start acting like a mother, that's when I'll treat her like one. Until then, fuck that bitch," I say.

"Well, I refuse to be around you as long you talk down on your mother. I know you're in pain," Mary says.

"Pain? You don't know what I'm going through right now. I just had to lay my brother down. It is way more than pain I am feeling. I swear I hope that nigga soul rot in hell for taking my brother away from me," I say as I interrupt Mary.

"Well, at least they got the dude who did it. I don't think they had to kill him, though," Mary says.

"Fuck that, we had to kill that nigga for Bobby," I slip up and say out of anger.

"What do mean *we*, Michael?" Mary says as she stops holding me, and I look at her, knowing I just confessed to being there when Adam was killed.

"Naw, I mean them," I try to hurry and switch my words.

"No, Michael, you said *we*! What did you do?" Mary asks.

I put my head down, knowing that she is not going to let it go.

"Okay. Me and some niggas found them niggas slippin' in the Crescents, and we got that nigga," I say.

"Oh my god! Michael, why would you do that?" Mary asks.

"What the fuck you mean why? Because that nigga killed my brother," I say.

"Yeah, I know that, but why did y'all have to shoot my cousin Isaiah? Now he paralyzed from the waist down, and his scholarship got denied because he can't play basketball anymore," Mary says, as she starts to get mad.

"Well, that nigga shouldn't have of been with that nigga Adam when he killed my brother," I say.

"This is not the Michael I love," Mary says as she covers her mouth.

"You love me?" I ask.

"I have always loved you ever since kindergarten," Mary explains.

"Why have you never said anything?" I ask.

"Because I didn't know if you felt the same way, and I didn't want to ruin our friendship," Mary says.

"Well, the crazy part is, I love you too, and I've always wanted to be with you but didn't know how to express my feelings toward you," I say.

Chapter 28

The Streets Be Talkin'

Ring! Ring! Ring!

"Yes, Mr. Stino," the voice on the phone says.

"So what's the news on the rest of them niggas that killed my nephew?" Stino asks.

"Now, now, now, Stino, we all know that's really not your nephew, more like your stepson," the voice on the phone says and laughs.

"Fuck you, nigga, I told you I got 10Gs for them nigga's heads," Stino says.

"Well, I heard one in jail. One is paralyzed, and the other one hasn't been seen since the shooting. People say he might of left to Texas," the voice on the phone says.

"Well, we gone have to find that nigga and make him pay for what he did," Stino says.

"You know they are just kids, right?" the voice on the phone says.

"Nigga, my lil nigga Bobby was just a kid, I don't give a fuck. Kid or not, them niggas want to play grown-man games. Well, I'm that Uncle Phil that will put these niggas in check over my nephews," Stino says.

"Okay, Big Papa, so what you tryna do to the nigga that's paralyzed? Kill him because I don't think there's much more you can do to him, he already gotta spend the rest of his life in a wheelchair," the voice on the phone says.

"Naw his life fucked already, I heard they revoked lil cuz scholarship to Duke so he suffered enough, but his brother gone pay. And what they talking 'bout with lil dude in jail?" Stino asks.

"They saying he is done for but offering lesser time if he snitch, but the lil nigga holding it down not saying shit so far," the voice on the phone says.

"Yeah, that's until that nigga get to the county, then that nigga gone be singing Beyoncé," Stino says.

"Yeah. You probably right about that, but I'ma put out the word for the brother, and I'll let you know what I find out," the voice on the phone says.

"Oh, I forgot to ask, what's the word on Adams murder? They find any suspects yet?" Stino asks.

"Nope, I guess that nigga Michael proved you wrong about how you thought he wasn't ready," the voice on the phone says.

"I would give him the credit if he had did it, but he wasn't the one who pulled the trigger," Stino explains.

"Damn, who was it then?" the voice on the phone asks.

"It was Lil D," Stino says.

"Wait, the little brother did it? What the fuck was he even doing there?" the voice on the phone asks.

"That nigga Michael said he needed to see the vengeance for Bobby but instead Lil D was the one who punished Adam," Stino says.

"Damn, that's deep. Ain't Michael the lil nigga that killed Big Adam back in the day?" the voice on the phone says.

"Yes, he was. I remember we had to take his body to the dead men creek and burned it in a barrel. That nigga was high as shit," Stino says.

"Yeah, thanks to you, that was the day you told him where David lived and that he had keys of dope there. I don't know if you notice but you cursed that family, no matter how you think you're helping them, you are just helping them die faster," the voice on the phone says.

"Nigga, fuck you! I swear you think you better than me, bitch. If it wasn't for me, you wouldn't be where you at. Remember that, nigga. And don't forget I wasn't the only one who saw David as a threat to our game plan. I was just the only one who cared about the rest of his family, so miss me with all that bullshit, nigga! You just call me when you got some more info, you goddamn snitch!" Stino says and hangs up the phone.

CHAPTER 29

THE STREETS BE TALKIN'

Ring! Ring! Ring!

"911 dispatch, what is your emergency?" dispatch asks.

"Yes, hi, I would like report a murder?" the voice on the phone says.

"What was that, dear? I could barely hear you," dispatch asks.

"I said I would like to report a murder," the voice on the other end of the phone says.

"Oh, dear Jesus! Are you okay? Are you hurt anywhere?" dispatch asks.

"No, ma'am, I'm okay. I'm calling regarding information on Adam's murder," the voice replies.

"Lord, you scared me! I thought you was near a murder scene. Okay. What information do you have?" dispatch says.

"I know who killed him," the voice asks.

"Do you have any evidence to prove your information?" dispatch asks.

"Yes, I do," the voice answers.

"What is your name, dear?" dispatch asks.

"I'm sorry, but I don't feel safe giving my name out," the voice says.

"Well, will you hold on for just few seconds and let me try to find someone who can better assist you?" dispatch says.

"Hey, Captain, we have a person on the phone who says they have information on that Adam's kid case, is officer Kane in?" dispatch yells out.

"No, he's not here, but I can help out," Officer Able steps up to say.

"Never mind, Captain!" dispatch yells out.

"What's their name?" Able asks.

"They are too scared to give it out, and it sounds like they are using a voice changer to cover up their voice, so I can't really tell if it's a man or woman," dispatch says.

"Okay. Hi, this is Officer Able, I'm hearing you can help us out with the murder suspect of Mr. Adam's case?" Able says.

"Yes, I know who did it," the voice on the phone says.

"Well, do you have any evidence to prove your statement?" Able says.

"Yes, I do, but I don't want anyone knowing I'm giving this information out, so is it possible for me to not be involved in this?" the voice says.

"That depends on what type of evidence you have," Able says.

"I have a recording of the person who killed him," the voice says.

"So you have the killing on video?" Able asks.

"No, I have the name of the guy who killed Adam," the voice answers.

"And what name would that be?" Able asks.

"His name is Michael, and he is from North Richmond," the voice answers.

"Are you talking about the older brother of Bobby who is also dead?" Able asks.

"Yes, that's him, and he is only older by five minutes," the voice says.

"How do you know so much about this family? You must be real close to them?" Able says.

"You can say that, but I just want justice for Adam because they didn't have to do him like that," the voice explains.

"So you're telling me Michael was the shooter? Why would he do that?" Able asks curiously.

"Because Adam was the one who killed Bobby, and he wanted revenge," the voice answers.

"Wait a minute, so you're telling me Adam is the killer of Bobby, and Bobby's brother is the killer of Adam?" Able says, trying to piece the puzzle together. He is surprised because one phone call just solved both cases.

"Yes, that's what I'm telling you. Now are you going to arrest Michael or what? Because I don't feel safe telling you all this, knowing he is out walking freely," the voice says.

"After I gather all the evidence you provide us and I properly investigate everything you just told me, I promise you that we will get justice for Adam's death, but in the meantime I'm going to need that recording to start my investigation. So where can we meet so I can start the process?" Able says.

"I don't think we should meet, I don't want to be exposed as the snitch," the voice says.

"Well, how about this. I promise to keep your name and face away from this case. You would only have to talk to me, no one else. Is that okay?" Able says.

"Will I have to testify in court?" the voice says.

"No, I will make sure you won't," Able says.

"Okay, we can meet at Nicole Park around the corner from the Richmond Police Station at seven, and I will give you the evidence you need to put that bitch away," the voice says.

"All right, I will see you then," Able says as he hangs up and runs down to the captain's office.

"Captain, I just solved both Bobby's and Adam's case," Able says with enthusiasm.

"I thought that was Officer Kane's case," Captain says with a bit confusion.

"Well, he is not here, and the witness only wants to talk to me," Able says with confidence.

"Well, I'll be damned. Your third week on the job, and you're already solving murders. Your last captain spoke highly of you, he said he could always count on you to get the job done, and I see what he means. But I still don't know why you would transfer to Richmond," Captain says.

"Thanks, Captain, and I have my reasons," Able responds.

"Well, I heard what happened to your baby girl, and I'm sorry for your loss," Captain says, trying to show empathy.

"No offense, Cap, but I'd rather not talk about it. Can we issue out a warrant on Michael?" Able asks.

"Isn't that Bobby older brother? Why would you want to do that?" Captain asks.

"Because my witness says he was the one who killed Adam in retaliation of killing his brother Bobby," Able says.

"Damn, these kids ain't got nothing better to do then going around killing each other! Just a waste of life," Captain says as he takes off his glasses and leans back in his chair."

"Yeah, tell me about it. That's all I used to see in Chicago," Able says.

"Okay, go to the judge and get the paperwork for the warrant, I sure hope your witness has good evidence because their Uncle Stino is a slick one. We been trying to get him for some years now, and going after his nephews won't be a pretty thing to do," Captain says with honesty.

"I promise you, Captain, it's going to put that young man away forever."

*****

Knock! Knock! Knock! Knock! Knock!

"Who the fuck banging on my damn door like they the fucking police!" Eve yells as she opens the door and notices it is in fact the police.

"What the fuck y'all want? Y'all found the niggas who killed my baby yet?" Eve asks as she takes a sip of Henney.

"Ma'am, is your son Michael here? We have an arrest warrant for the murder of Adam," Officer Able says.

128

"Who the fuck is Adam? And naw that nigga ain't here," Eve says in a slurred language.

"May we come in and check for ourselves?" Able says as him and five other police officers go through the door and search for Michael.

"Ma'am, where is your son? He is in a lot of trouble, and it would be in your best interest to turn him over to the police," Able says.

"Motherfucker, I don't know where he at. Do I look like that nigga mama?" Eve says, taking another sip.

"Check the bedrooms, check everywhere. Make sure he's not hiding in no closets or the bathrooms!" Able yells out.

"You want to come check my bedroom, Officer? I'll be more than happy to give yo white ass a tour," Eve says, lifting her skirt and showing her legs off.

"No, ma'am, I don't," Able says as he looks disgusted.

"What's wrong, sugar? Never had some real coffee in your life before?" Eve says as she moves one of her shoulder straps off her shoulder.

"Nope! I haven't, I probably never will drink coffee ever again. Have y'all found anything?" Able says as he starts to get uncomfortable.

"I told y'all asses he ain't here," Eve says, taking another drink and sparking up a blunt.

"Ma'am, do you have recommendation for that marijuana?" Able asks.

"Yeah, don't buy it from Ricky, his shit taste like bamma. If you want that dope shit, go to Redman on 6th Street, his shit get you high as fuck," Eve says as she starts to laugh and blows smoke in the officer's face.

"Let's get out of here, y'all. Ma'am, if you see your son, tell him to turn himself in so he doesn't make matters worse than what they are," Able says.

"Yes, Sir Officer, and this coffee will be hot and ready for you whenever you man up," Eve says as she hangs on the door in a slutty way.

Officer Able gets the chills, and his body shakes with disgust.

"Let's get the hell out of here," Able says as him and the other officers speed walk back to their cars.

*****

Ring! Ring! Ring!
"Hello?" I say.
"Boy, where the fuck you at?" Eve asks.
"I just picked Donny up from school, and we on our way to the house," I say.
"So who the fuck did you kill?" Eve asks.
"Are you drunk, Mom?" I say, trying to switch the subject.
"Yes, the fuck I am, but that still don't answer my fucking question. Now who the fuck did you kill?" Eve says.
"I ain't kill nobody, what the fuck are you talking about?" I say.
"Boy! Don't you talk to me that type of way, I am your mother," Eve warns.
"Then act like it," I respond back.
"If I didn't act like it, then I would've told the cops that just busted down my door with an arrest warrant for you where you was," Eve says.
"What are you talking about? Arrest warrant for what?" I say.
"Nigga, I just said for murder, they said you killed somebody. Now tell me who the fuck you killed," Eve says.
I get nervous and start to think on how the police found out about the killing.
"Mom, I ain't killed nobody, I promise," I say.
"Nigga, I can hear it in your voice that you're lying, so tell me now, or I can't help you," Eve says as she takes a sip of her drink.
I take a deep breath to think about what I'm gonna say. "I killed the nigga that killed Bobby," I say.
"What the fuck you say?" Eve says as she spits out her drink.
"I said I got revenge for my brother," I say.
"So that bitch-ass nigga who killed my baby is dead? And you killed him?" Eve asks.
"Yes, Mama, I did," I say.

"Boy, I'm so proud of you, maybe you are your dad's son after all," Eve says.

*****

Blur...blur...blur...blur... The police car pulls up behind me and Donny.

"What's that?" Eve asks.

"Mama, you told the police where I was?" I asks.

"How the hell I'ma do that, when I didn't even know where y'all was. But yo ass better run before they get yo ass," Eve says.

"And what? Leave my brother so they can take him? I'll be damned if I let him go to jail for my mistakes," I say.

"Put your hands in the air and drop the phone. Dispatch, do you copy?" a cop hops out his car with his gun drawn down on me and Donny.

"Dispatch, here, go ahead," dispatch says through the radio.

"I have the suspects here that match the description of the warrant that was passed around. I'm in need of backup," the cop responds on his walkie-talkie.

"Copy that. Backup is in pursuit, be advised that the suspects are armed and dangerous," dispatch says.

"Copy that, dispatch. All right, you little niggers, get on your knees and place yours hands behind your back," the cop yells.

"Man, for what? We ain't even do nothing!" I yell and say.

"I'm not gonna repeat myself, get your asses on the ground now!" the cop yells again.

Blur... Blur... Another cop car pulls up.

"Officer Able, thanks for assisting," the cop says.

"No problem, we only need the older one. The younger one can go home," Able orders.

"Michael, I want you to back up slowly and lay flat on the ground with your hands behind your back and your legs crossed!" Able yells out.

"Donny, I'ma need you to run straight home, and don't tell anyone. And I mean not even Mama, what really happened, do you hear me?" I say.

"Yes, bro"! Lil D says as he starts to cry.

"Don't cry, bro, I told you I would always protect you no matter what. I love you, little nigga, and remember be better than me and Bobby ever was and try to break our family curse. Now go!" I say.

"Okay, bro, I love you!" Lil D says.

"Mr. Michael, you are under arrest for the murder of Adam. You have the right to remain silent. Anything you say can be held against you in court. You have a right to an attorney, if you refuse those rights," Able says.

"Man, I know my rights. Miss me with all that shit," I say as they put handcuffs on me and stuff me in the back of the police car.

About the Author

Tyvon Price is a young black male who survived the streets of Richmond, California. He dreams on bringing back the hope and dreams of other young people who have survived the struggle of the hood environment. He wants a better life for his family and for the generations yet to come. He is set to become the curse breaker over his family.

CPSIA information can be obtained
at www.ICGtesting.com
Printed in the USA
LVHW091051141220
674117LV00009B/143

9 781645 442622